Madonna Swan
A Lakota Woman's Story

MADONNA SWAN

SWAN

A LAKOTA

WOMAN'S

STORY

as told through
Mark St. Pierre

UNIVERSITY OF OKLAHOMA PRESS
NORMAN AND LONDON

Dedicated

To friends in deed Roberta and James.
In honor of all people who have suffered with the stigma
of "Incurable Contagious Disease"

Library of Congress Cataloging-in-Publication Data

St. Pierre, Mark, 1950–
Madonna Swan : a Lakota woman's story / as told through
Mark St. Pierre.
p. cm.
Includes bibliographical references and index.
ISBN 0–8061–2369–9
1. Swan, Madonna, 1928– . 2. Dakota Indians—Biography.
3. Dakota Indians—Social life and customs. 4. Tuberculosis—
Patients—Biography. I. Title.
E99.D1S937 1991
973'.0497502—dc20
[B] 91–50306

The paper in this book meets the guidelines for permanence
and durability of the Committee on Production Guidelines for
Book Longevity of the Council on Library Resources, Inc.∞

All photographs are from the collection of Madonna Swan.
Maps are by Deborah Reade.

Contents

Preface

DESPITE THE passage of many years since the completion of the first drafts, reading the simple words in this collection still deeply moves me. This emotion is partly an outgrowth of the honest relationship Madonna Swan and I developed during our frequent interviews, but more, I suspect, a result of this Native American woman's keen ability to teach us—perhaps in a way we've never known—the twentieth-century experience.

I became familiar with Madonna through her mother, a Lakota elder respected for her knowledge of Lakota lifeways. Madonna was a Head Start teacher at the time. As we became acquainted, I was fascinated by her personal qualities and strength of character. After having heard these stories in casual conversation over many years, I decided they needed to be shared, particularly with young Lakota people who had been presented in literature with few twentieth-century role models.

Between 1975 and 1981 I recorded triplicate versions of these stories, and in the writing process edited the stories into a unified vignette, pulling the best aspects from the three versions. My next challenge was to add settings where needed and to write them in such a manner that the colloquial manner of the telling was left intact and had the proper mood and feeling.

The stories were then arranged in a loose chronological order, creating the sense of a story line. In some cases the time and place of the original telling was lost, such as in stories from her grandmother and mother, so I put them into the book where I thought they would be appropriate or poignant.

All of the stories seemed to have the common link of Lakota irony, wisdom, and humor. Where necessary, this quality was enhanced by adding something she might have said during a different interview at the end of the story.

Madonna's narrative rings of honesty and caring, over-riding the impact of her early reservation life.

In this recounting of memories from three generations of Indian women, *Madonna Swan: A Lakota Woman's Story* be-comes a clear window on an obscure yet deeply significant history. Beginning with the stories of Julia Brave Eagle, born in 1860, which offer insight into the tragedy of the con-quest and the adjustment to reservation confinement, and continuing through those of her daughter Lucy High Pine-Swan, born in 1900, whose legacy straddles the closing days of Indian power and freedom, to the modern chronicles of Madonna herself, *Madonna Swan: A Lakota Woman's Story* becomes far more than a mere remembrance of a tribal past. It is a story of life, dreams, and human yearnings.

Further, this collection serves as a tribute to all those Native Americans who survived tuberculosis, as Madonna did, and represents a closing and healing of that terrible wound in Lakota and human history, a period darkened by the sheer magnitude of an epidemic whose impact on tribal societies has been largely overlooked in Native American literature.

In Madonna's story we find the sometimes sad, some-times heartwarming connection between her own Indian world and the white world in which she often lived and worked. Born on the Cheyenne River Reservation to the Lakota people, or Western Sioux, Madonna was sur-rounded by the adjustments of Indian peoples to the open-ing of the reservations and the declaration of citizenship for all Native Americans—an event that, above all, fash-ioned the views this woman so eloquently presents.

In her world the "ghost dance" was but a memory clouded by Christian missionaries' and federal agents' ef-forts to obliterate traditional expressions of Indian spiri-tualism. Through it all comes Madonna's chilling tale of confinement for ten years in a tuberculosis sanitorium, sur-rounded by death, dealing with her own suffering, fighting for survival. Finally, after she became the first person in America to undergo experimental lung-removal surgery, her life was saved, along with the lives of many other TB victims, Indian and white.

Madonna tells of her health, her years as a jeweler, her admission to college, and her ten years as a Head Start teacher, and her life, as an embodiment of Sioux values, affirms the fact that folk values and culture have positive value to today's subjugated minorities.

Here is a true life story of a modern Lakota woman, faithful to her culture and her generation. But at the same time we witness the emergence of a unique and powerful heroine who transcends deep-rooted culture, offering a testament to the universality of the human condition and the meaning of raw human courage.

MARK ST. PIERRE

Steamboat Springs, Colorado

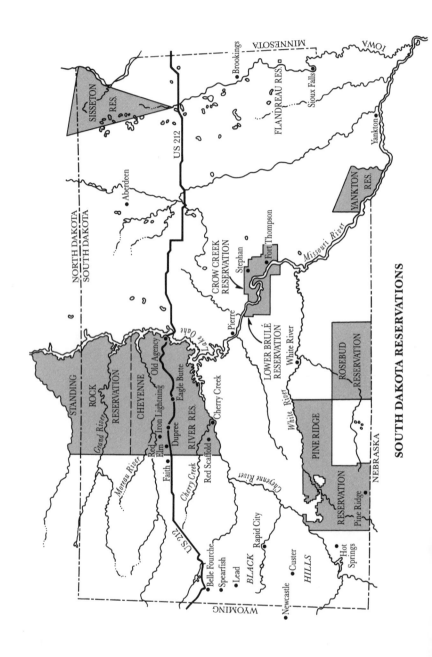

SOUTH DAKOTA RESERVATIONS

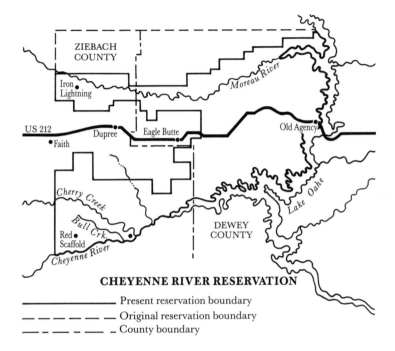

ZIEBACH
COUNTY

Iron
Lightning

Moreau River

US 212

Dupree   Eagle Butte   Old Agency

•Faith

Cherry Creek

Bull Crk.

Red
Scaffold
Cheyenne River

DEWEY
COUNTY

Lake Oahe

CHEYENNE RIVER RESERVATION

———————— Present reservation boundary
— — — — — Original reservation boundary
— — — — — County boundary

Part One

THE SOUND OF PRAISE

I, MADONNA MARY SWAN ABDALLA, was born to the union of James Hart Swan and Lucy Josephine High Pine-Swan, September 12, 1928. I was the fifth child of the ten children born to this family. Only five of the ten children survived until adulthood. Manuel, the oldest, was born in 1919. He was a healthy baby, and one year after his birth, Mom had a big giveaway to honor her firstborn.[1] She gave away a tipi, beaded cradleboards, saddlebags, horses, Pendleton blankets, and many quilts.[2] She gave away everything she had been given to start her married life.

Shirley Suzzana was born in 1921 but died of pneumonia later that same year. Kermit Joseph was born in 1924 and died of a wound received during World War II.

Austin Paul was born in 1926 and died of a head injury at four years old. He fell off a bed at Grandmother High Pine's place on the White River. Austin got sick after the fall, and his stomach got bigger and bigger. Mom and Grandma tried to give him an enema, but he got worse. By the time they got him to the hospital in Rosebud, it was too late. He died later that night.

Shirley Monica was born in 1930. Orby was born in 1932 and died as a teenager. He suffered from cerebral palsy, but he was a very bright boy and very close to Mom. Martha Mary was born in 1934 and died the next day. The last female child born to my parents was Ivy Lucy, born in 1942. She died in infancy.[3] Erskin Elias, my mother's last child, was born in 1944, and he still lives in Cherry Creek.

From the children that died, it might seem that we had it very bad, but we didn't. We were born to a very strong mother whose love and patience more than made up for everything we went without. My dad finished high school at Chilocco Indian School and took two years postgraduate work at Lawrence, Kansas.[4] He had more education than any man of his generation and always stressed the importance of using our minds. Dad had his problems, but he always seemed to provide for us in the way of food, clothes, and school supplies.

Grandpa Puts On His Shoes

MY EARLIEST memories were of those years we lived in Iron Lightning community, with my grandfather, Puts On His Shoes. His land was north of the trading post at Red Elm, South Dakota. The government had built him a frame house when the reservation was settled many years earlier. They called these little frame houses "chief's houses" because they had been built for important men.[5] The frame house had a kitchen, a bedroom, and a large room upstairs. That is where my father and mother, my brothers Kermit and Manuel, my sister Shirley, and I lived. We all lived with my grandfather and were happy there.

Puts On His Shoes was a good man, but he drank a lot, because he had many white friends he did business and drank with. Grandpa Puts, we called him, was alone then. His wife had passed away many years earlier, and he had no children still living. So he drank quite a bit, but he never got into trouble. He never fought anyone or was put in jail. Usually, he was a kind and wise man, a good grandfather. He lived a long life.

I don't know when he was born, but it was before there were the reservations. He was an old warrior, an old-fashioned Indian, what the white people called a chief. Grandpa Puts told us many stories of the old times when the Lakota people were free.

Memories of Old-Timers

WHEN I WAS a little girl, many of the old people who had lived before the reservations were still among us. They were different from people living now.[6] They were stately people who carried themselves and spoke with respect all the time, even to white people. My grandfather was one of those old-timers. He told us many times, "Never trust a white man," but he didn't dislike all white people and had friends who were white. They spoke with him in Indian because he spoke no English.

Grandpa was a thin man and always wore a chief's blanket, its wide beaded strip around his middle. His hair was black mixed with silver and was always wrapped with rags or wool strips. He wore white man's pants but never owned a pair of shoes; he always wore moccasins.

One day Grandfather took us for a long walk. We gathered parts of different plants. As we went along, Grandfather explained how they were used. When we got back to the house, Grandpa took some of the leaves and boiled them like tea. Then he washed his hair with this and told us if we did this, our hair would always be thick and black like his. Grandpa showed us how to gather red willow and strip and chop it up to make tobacco mixings. He had no white man's education but was a very wise man.

Grandpa never went to Christian church. He always prayed with his pipe and took sweat baths.[7] I never knew what that little hut that stood off from the main house was for. I was very young then and just starting to remember and understand the things that I saw and the things people told me.

One day these two old men, Lone Eagle and Jake Bull Eagle, came to sweat with Grandpa Puts On His Shoes.[8] Soon another old man named Swift Bear joined them. They visited and drank coffee. Late in the afternoon they headed down the hill towards a flat place where the sweat lodge stood. The old men gathered wood and stones and covered the sweat lodge with an old buffalo robe and quilts.

I asked Mom, "What are those men going to do?"

She replied, "They are going to take a sweat bath. One of those men has not been feeling well, and they are going to pray to the Grandfathers to find out what is wrong with him."

"When are they going to do that?" I asked.

"Probably this evening at dusk," she said, and went on peeling and braiding the wild turnips she had dug that morning.[9]

The men didn't have their sweat bath that night. As Mom fed them, I overheard one of them say they couldn't have the sweat until another person arrived. I asked Mom what they were waiting for.

"They are waiting for a virgin, either a boy or a young woman, who must carry the rocks into the sweat bath so everything will go well for the sick man they are praying for.[10] They are waiting for Swift Bear's granddaughter."

Swift Bear's granddaughter came that evening, and they had the sweat bath the next day. When they were finished and eating a feast Mom had prepared, I asked Grandpa, "Lala, why did you wait for Swift Bear's grand-daughter?"

He answered, "Not everybody or just anybody can bring those rocks in there. You must approach sacred things in the right way. We needed a virgin to help us."

"What is a virgin?" I asked.

He replied, "It is a man who has not taken a woman, or a woman who has not been with a man. All things must be done properly if you are to gain benefit from these ceremonies."[11] Grandpa taught us a lot. He liked to talk about religion and ceremonies, about the proper way to approach these things and the grandfathers in heaven.[12]

Later that summer, I remember, Mom pitched Chief William White Swan's tipi.[13] White Swan was my dad's father; he died long before I was born. White Swan was Grandpa Puts's brother. Puts used to put that tipi up every summer. I guess he did it to remember and honor his brother. The tipi was made of buffalo hide and was a chief's tipi, so the smoke flaps were painted black. On either side of the door were painted figures of horses and buffalos. Inside, Grandpa placed some old buffalo robes

and willow back rests. He stayed in there for about a
month.[14] When visitors came, they would go in there and
smoke and visit with Grandpa. They spoke a lot of the old
days, but I never remember them talking about battles.
Sometimes the old men would get into a heated debate
about one thing or another, yet always they were friendly
when it was over. They said things to each other in harsh
words; still, they never swore. They seemed to understand
that it takes discussion and argument to make decisions or
get along. Today the slightest disagreement, and some
people will pout for weeks or even months. People think
that to argue or debate is not Indian. That is not true.

                            Dust Bowl

IN 1933 very little rain came. It had been this way for
quite a while, I think. The ground was bone dry, and the
berry bushes produced nothing that year. Sometimes great
clouds of dust would blow, and the sky would get dark.
Grandfather Puts On His Shoes said this was very bad and
that a sun dance should be held to break the drought. I've
heard that sun dances were held on other reservations to
break the very bad weather.[15]
     The drought affected everyone, white and Indian alike.
One day my grandfather took us to the town of Faith,
South Dakota. When we got to town, we noticed a large
crowd gathered on the south side of town, out on the prairie. We went over there, and here a great big hole had been
dug. There were a lot of men and cattle near the hole.
They were shooting their cattle and throwing the cattle
into the hole. Grandpa went to ask one of his white friends
why they were doing this. "There is no feed or water. The
cattle are starving to death. We can't stand to see them suf-
fer any more," the white man spoke in Indian. "You and
your family can butcher as many as you want. They are not
diseased, just starving."

We camped north of the railroad depot. Soon Dad
came with the other wagon. Grandpa walked over to the
wagon and said, "Nephew, these white men are killing
their herds because there is no more feed or water around
here. They said we could butcher as many as we want." My
dad was kind of funny about certain things. If someone
brought a deer or an antelope to the house to give us, he
wouldn't eat it. My dad believed that deer were put on the
earth for the sake of beauty, not to be eaten.[16] So anyway,
Grandpa kept telling Dad to go over and get some meat.
"I'll even butcher it for you," Grandpa said, but Dad didn't
want any.

Other families, like the Knifes and Lone Eagles, were
there, and they were butchering, so they gave Mom some
big pieces of meat to jerk. We got some meat anyway, and
Grandpa got some soup. The Knifes are related to us
through Grandpa Puts On His Shoes's family.

🐾   *Leaving Iron Lightning and Grandpa*

LATE IN THE summer of 1933 my father had decided to
move back to his home community of Cherry Creek. Because Puts On His Shoes was my father's uncle, brother to
White Swan, in the Indian way he was my dad's father also.
Grandpa did not want us to move. He told my father that
if he stayed he could have the land and the house for his
own and whichever of the horses he wanted. Still, Dad was
determined to leave. We hated to go; we loved Grandpa
Puts. He had always been kind and gentle towards us,
bringing candy and telling us stories.

When Dad told Grandpa we were leaving for sure,
Grandpa was very sad, but he was a true man. He said, "If
you wish to leave and your mind cannot be changed, then
I'll give you a wagon and some horses for the trip. I have
no son, and when I leave this earth, this land and house
will be yours also." He must have given my dad and broth-

ers twenty horses all together. Among them were mares, geldings, saddle horses, and a team and wagon. He gave these to us, so we had two wagons, an old one and the new one Grandpa had given us.[17]

When the day came, Mom and Dad loaded the wagons. It was a hot day late in August. Grandpa said, "Make sure you leave room for my brother White Swan's tipi. I am afraid if something should happen to me, no one would care for it. I am too old to put it up any more."[18]

Dad said, "We don't have room for it. I will come back after it." So we left it, and that was the last we saw of White Swan's tipi.

When we were in the wagons, ready to leave, Grandfather shook our hands, then he took our hands in his, and holding us like that he said, "Be brave and always pray every day to Wakon Tonka, because he is our great helper and will be throughout your life." He went on to say, "Never trust a white man behind your back! They will stab you, in one way or another!"

Grandfather had been through the wars and the troubles and knew what he was talking about. We were ready to leave, so Kermit and Manuel saddled two ponies and started to run the other horses ahead of us. We said our last goodbyes and started on our journey to Cherry Creek. Mom drove one team and wagon, my dad the other.

We traveled three days, first camping at Faith overnight. Early the next day the wagons started out again. That night our family camped in Red Scaffold.[19] We stayed there overnight, then started out across the prairie the next morning, towards my Uncle Frank Council Bear's home. He lived on Bull Creek, west of Cherry Creek.[20] We stopped to rest and fix lunch near Felix Creek a few miles from my uncle's place. Mom was going to start a fire and make tea and coffee. We had our lunch with us, boiled eggs, potatoes, and bread. Our plan was to eat quickly and get moving again.

The boys ate first because Dad told them, "Go ahead and eat; then drive the horses to Uncle Frank's place and wait for us there." It was a very windy day, so we rode down into a draw, a sheltered place out of the wind. Mom built a fire and made coffee and tea, and here, that fire got away! It started burning the dry grass. We had started a prairie fire! My father took both of the wagons across the creek and put them on the north side with us smaller kids inside. Next, he moved all of the horses over there also. Mom, Dad, and my two brothers began to fight the fire with spades and shovels, using them to swat the fire and dig a fire break. They moved in a circle around the fire, yet by the time they put it out, it must have burned at least five acres! It was late in the afternoon when they got the fire out and we finally ate our lunch.

We finished lunch and started our journey again. That evening we got to my uncle's place, down on Bull Creek near the Cheyenne River. Uncle Frank was very glad to see us and said we should stay with them.

 Killing the Wolf

WE LIKED LIVING with our aunt and uncle on Bull Creek. There were more women to help with the house chores, so we got to spend more time with Mom.[21] She liked to go out and sit in the evenings after supper. We girls would sometimes follow her. Mom would relax and turn her face towards the sun. She looked so pretty like that. Us kids would beg her to tell us a story. She would tease us back, saying, "No, you don't want to hear one of those old stories again, do you?"

"Sure we do."

"Well, okay then," and she started.[22]

"When I was eight or nine years old, and my little brother Thomas was four, my brothers Henry and George were also there. We lived in a tent.[23] It was a big wall tent, so inside was a cook stove and wood heater. The tent had a liner to keep us warm. My mother and father and the baby slept in a double bed in the northeast corner. That's where Mom slept even on nights when Dad was not home, like that night. Right next to theirs was my bed, standing east to west. On the other end of the tent there was another bed, and that was where my two brothers were sleeping.

"We were all asleep, but my mother, your grandmother, thought she heard something. She was listening, and here, something was eating real loud. In the dim moonlight, there was a wolf in our tent! She reached her hand over to me and woke me up. She told me, 'Something is eating at the stove, and I'm going to kill it. Grab your little brother here and wake Tom and George. All of you sit on the boys' bed.' Then she gave me a big piece of rawhide for a shield and waited for us to move. I was really scared. Mom picked up another piece of rawhide, for a shield, and an axe. When we were all ready, we sat there hardly breathing.

"That animal must have been really hungry, because it didn't even hear all this going on. Mom moved very slowly and went around behind it, then hit it very hard on the head. There was a loud yelp! That was all.[24] It just fell over dead. Mom told me to light a lamp, and here, she had killed a great big wolf! We all looked at it. Then Mom drug it by the tail, and she dropped it a little ways from our tent.

"The next morning I got up, got dressed, went out, and there it was, still lying there, so I called my brothers to come see it. My brother George looked at it and said he was going to ride into White River and tell the storekeeper.[25] So he rode over there and told him about it. He was the only white man who lived near us then. The storekeeper went to Rosebud and told the farm agent to come look at it. The farm agent came over and took a picture of Grandma with the wolf.[26] The picture was in the Episcopal newsletter called *Anpo Win* (Dawn Woman)!"

Grandma High Pine was visiting us that summer, and she had been sitting there listening quietly, smiling to herself.

"Is it true, Grandma? Did you kill that wolf?" Manuel asked.

"Sure, it's true! That wolf was old and deaf like I

am now," she said.[27] We laughed and laughed. Finally,
Grandma couldn't hold it in any more, and she laughed
with us.

                                    Inyan Hoksila

THAT SUMMER of 1934 I was six years old. It was a good
summer, full of happy times. We moved from Council
Bear's place because Dad had gotten a job as a police officer
in that district. Grandma High Pine spent every spare moment she had gathering turnips and berries. There still
weren't very many, but it was not as dry as it had been the
summer before. That summer Mom and Dad went on a
buffalo hunt. They were looking for strays that had gotten
away from a Mr. Phillips, who had sold his herd to the state
because of the drought.[28]

Grandma loved us, and she would rub our backs, hug
us, and tell us that she hoped we never grew up. We would
hug her and tell her that we promised to stay small. Then
she would tell us a story. On this day it was a story that her
mother had told her.

"I will tell you this story of Inyan Hoksila (Rock Boy).[29]
He is one of the spiritual ancestors of the Lakota people.
I believe these stories. That is why I pray with the pipe,
like an Indian, because I was taught with stories like
this one.

"There was a village where two young and very pretty,
but also very foolish, girls lived. The two girls were told
they should not go walking out alone at night. They should
always be with an older female relative. One night the girls
decided to go out alone, unescorted. They were laying
against a tipi, looking at the stars. One of the girls turned
to the other and said, 'You look at the brightest star you
can find and pretend it is your husband. I'll find a bright
star and pretend it is my husband. Then you show me your
husband, and I will show you mine, and we will see whose

is the most handsome.' They lay talking this way for a long time, when one of the girls said she was getting sleepy and said she was going back to her tipi and go to sleep. The other girl said she would do the same.

"They went to bed, but when they awoke they noticed something very strange. The older girl saw a man laying next to her in the lodge. She knew it was not her parents' lodge. Frightened, she got up and looked outside. She saw that it was a very strange land she was in. It was much like home, with tipis and people walking about, but the people were dressed in very beautiful clothes! The girl sat down thinking and wondering how she had gotten so far from her mother and father. She saw another tipi a little ways off, and from inside that tent came her girlfriend from home. She walked over to her and asked where they were. 'I don't know. Maybe we are in another world. It looks so strange here. And I woke up next to a strange man!'

'So did I, and I'm lonely for home.'

"The two girls hugged each other and cried. 'Do you suppose we got our wish?' the younger one finally asked.

'I don't know, but it seems like it!' They spoke to each other for some time, not knowing what to do or say. Soon the older girl said, 'Well I guess I better go home and cook for that man.' The older girl woke up her new husband and said, 'Come, we will eat together.' She asked her husband where they were.

'You were looking at the sky world and wishing for a husband, and this is where you are,' he said.

'But I am lonely for my people. I don't want to stay here,' she said, and began to cry.

'Do not cry, it will do you no good. I am your husband now, and you will never be allowed to return to your people. There are a lot of women in this camp. You should get to know some, and you will not be lonely any more. You can go with them to gather berries and wild turnips. The men are going on a hunt and will bring back meat and robes for you to tan,' he said.

"So the girl went visiting and drank tea with her new

neighbors. That night her man came back with a deer. So it went, on and on, but the two girls were very lonely for their homeland and relatives. One day they were to go turnip digging. Their men told the girls, 'You can gather as many turnips as you like, except *hu blaska* [false turnips].[30] You must never pick that!' The girl went over to her friend's lodge and asked if she was ready to go.

'Yes, but my man told me something very strange. He told me I could go gather as many turnips as I wanted, but I was not to dig the hu blaska. He would not tell me why,' she said.

'My man told me the same thing, and he would not tell me why, either.'

"They were digging turnips only a short time when they came upon a hu blaska. The younger girl said, 'Let's not dig it.' But the older girl said, 'Let's find out why we are not supposed to dig, by pulling it up!' The girls dug and dug and pulled the turnip three times. On the fourth try it came out.

"The hu blaska has no turnip, only a long root. That is why it is called false turnip. When the girls pulled it out, it had a very thick, long root; and when it came out, it made a hole in the ground. They lay down and looked through the hole. Very surprised, they saw their earth village below. Seeing this made them very lonely. Over the next few weeks they started saving rawhide to make a rope they could use to climb back down to earth.

"They did this a long time, and one day they decided to try to get back to the earth. That day the men went hunting, so the girls had their chance. The girls returned to the hu blaska. They pulled it up, and the hole was still there, so they dropped the rawhide rope down towards the earth. The rope dropped through the clouds, so they could not see if it reached the earth.

"The older girl tied the rope around her waist and the other end to a stake in the ground. She lowered herself down through the hole. She began the long climb down through the clouds towards the earth. Soon she found the rope was too short, and she hung there, halfway between heaven and earth.

"She cried out for the other girl to pull her back up. She was pregnant and too heavy and too weak to pull herself back up. The other girl said, 'You are too heavy for me to pull you up!' Finally, the older girl begged her friend to cut the rope. The rope was cut, and she fell to the earth and was killed.

"People in her village on earth had seen her hanging there and ran to the spot where she had fallen. When they found her, she was dead, but the baby still moved inside her. They cut her open and took a baby boy out. They put the woman on a scaffold, then took the baby back to the parents of the dead woman. Those old people raised the baby as their own.

"The boy was different from the other children of the village. He grew very quickly and was very bright and really strong! When the boys would climb trees, this strange boy would climb the biggest tree faster than any one of his friends.

"One time this boy went sliding with some boys from the village. The boys took their buffalo-rib sleds and climbed a tall hill.[31] The boys told their strange friend to ride last on the sled, and here, the boy said, 'No! I should ride first!', but the boys would not listen to him and made him ride last. On the way down the hill they hit a rough spot and spilled. The strange boy rolled over the other boys and killed them.[32] When the mourning parents questioned him, he said, 'I am Inyan Hoksila, Rock Boy. I am not like you; I am from the other world. My father is from the sky world.'

"He grew up to be an exceptional man in every way and became an ancestor of the Lakota people. So you see, you shouldn't be boy crazy when you grow up. You can see what became of those girls!"

Grandma put her hand over her mouth and just

laughed and laughed. She would always be telling us stories like that to make us laugh and to teach us something.

                           Moving to Cherry Creek

MY FATHER worked that spring and summer in Bridger,
but he had bought a house near Cherry Creek and had an
addition built on it, so it was a big house. That was where
we moved in the fall of 1934, so our journey was done.

Because we were living out in the country then, my
brothers were my first real playmates. A little later that fall
my cousin Mary Council Bear moved near us, so I sometimes got to play with her, and enjoyed that very much. We
had some white neighbors that lived out in the country
near us. They would come and play with us, too.[33] They
usually brought milk and eggs with them. Their mom
would always send a note for our mom, asking her to send
a prairie chicken or cottontail in return for the eggs. This
made it nice for us, because we needed the milk and eggs,
and my brothers were always hunting for something!

It seemed Mom always had a good garden.[34] She watered it by hauling many loads of water up from the river.
Mom would hitch the team and wagon, then haul large tins
and barrels. While Mom was filling her containers, we
would play along the river. Our favorite was to pick up
round flat rocks, looking for just the right one to skip or
throw at fish or whatever we liked. Shirley and I played all
sorts of things on these trips, mostly using our imaginations. I don't remember having candy, but we would make
Kool-Aid and drink nectar or pop in those days. For a treat
Mom would make us cookies or popcorn. These were the
only kinds of treats we had back then.

Sundays were always a happy and interesting day for
me. Dad would take time to talk to us on Sundays or other
family occasions. He would read the Bible, and Grandma
High Pine would pray with her pipe. Dad would often pick

out a scripture and relate it to our modern situation. He would use these times to teach us a lesson about people or life.

Even at an early age we were responsible for certain chores. We brushed our hair, braided it, and helped make breakfast with Mom or Grandma. Mom told us early in life how to do the dishes, not to let the food harden on the plates or they would be much harder to wash.

We all lived in one big room in the log house. Grandma had her own little cabin. We'd stop in and visit her on the way back from feeding the chickens. Later in the day we would make our beds. Often we would haul the bedding outdoors to air them out. Unlike some folks, we all had our own bed and headboards.[35]

There was a time when we all learned to make our own mattresses. The wool came in big, tight gunny sacks. They were stuffed really hard, and it was hard for our small hands to pull the gray dusty wool from the sacks. The dust from the wool was giving us sore throats so Kermit tied handkerchiefs around our mouths and noses. That really helped a lot. After we pulled it out, we washed and dried it, then stuffed the mattresses.

It seemed that in those days we did most things for ourselves. Our best dresses were all handmade from calico, our play dresses from cotton flour sacking. Although we had little, it did not seem we wanted for much, and it often seemed as if we had it better than many other people around us; we were happy then.

                    Lucy Goes to School

THAT FALL I started school in Cherry Creek at the day school.[36] My brothers complained that they did not want me to go to school there. They told Mom and Dad that I cried a lot, and it embarrassed them and made them feel bad, so they didn't want me to go to school there any more.

I suppose I cried because I wanted to be home with Mom, but I can't really remember.

I was scared to go to school in the first place; now they were talking about sending me to Immaculate Conception, a Catholic boarding school at Stephan, South Dakota, far from home.[37] Mom took me aside and told me not to cry. She dried my tears and said, "I wish I had more school. You are a very smart little girl, and you could go as far with your education as you want."

"And even be a nurse?" I asked.

"Yes, and even be a nurse, if that's what you want," she said.

"Let me tell you why I couldn't go to school when I was little. When I was a little girl, I would sometimes die.[38] When I was dead and then came back to life, I could not remember anything. Some of the other girls were going to school. I couldn't because of these times when I would die or faint or whatever it would be called now. When I was ten years old, I wished very much that I could go to school and learn like the other girls. I talked to my mom about it, and she talked to Dad.

"One summer day not long after that, we were swimming and splashing in the creek and playing 'move the village' games. I heard Dad calling, so we raced back towards the log house. I was ahead because I was the fastest runner even though I was younger. Before I reached the house, my heart felt like it stopped, and I fell dead. My sister Mary told me later what happened next.

"My dad picked me up and carried me to a spot beside the house; then he sent my older brother to bring Mrs. Thin Elk, Dad's sister-in-law. We were kind of afraid of her because she was said to have a lot of power,[39] the kind the Catholic priest warned us to stay away from. My parents used to tell us not to be afraid of her because she was a good old woman who could cure the sick and had never hurt anyone. Still, we would make up witch stories about her and run when she came.

"Mrs. Thin Elk came quickly; she told my dad to spread a white muslin on the floor of his summer tipi and then to lay me down on top of it. She said she would try and find the problem. All the children were sent away; just the adults came into the lodge. Mary, my sister, was peeking under the tipi cover.

"The old woman told my father to sing and fill his pipe. When he was finished, she had him stand near me and point the pipe at me. Mrs. Thin Elk took her little parfleche satchel and opened it. She took out a piece of red flannel and laid a buffalo horn and a bundle of sage on it. Then the old woman began to pray. As she prayed, she brushed my head and neck with the bunch of sage and then my body. Next, she stood up and sang to the east. When she sang, her chest made a noise like a bird singing. Then she picked up a handful of grey dust, and when she blew it out of her hand, it was yellow. Next, she sang to the south; again, the bird noise came from her chest, and she picked up the earth; and when she blew, black dust came out of her hand. Then, to the west she sang and blew the dust. This time red dust came out. Finally, to the north she sang, that bird noise coming from nowhere, and the grey dust came out as white dust.[40]

"Mary told me later that she was really scared, but she was too amazed to leave. As she watched, the old lady bent down over me and turned me on my side. Making a loud noise like a buffalo, she put the buffalo horn on my neck and sucked. Very soon she asked for a white piece of buckskin. When Mom brought it, Mrs. Thin Elk tipped the horn onto the buckskin, and a red blood clot came out. She told my dad that this was causing all the problems and that I would never "die" like that again.[41] Then she said to get a frog. My dad had seen Mary peeking around, so he sent her to get a big frog from the creek. Mary ran to our swimming place and was soon back with a frog. Mary didn't exactly see what Mrs. Thin Elk did with the frog, but she wrapped it and the blood clot up in that buckskin and told Dad to place it on a high hill. Then they smoked Dad's pipe.

"When I woke up, Dad gave Mrs. Thin Elk a horse to take home. Mom gave her a pretty shawl with flowers embroidered on it.[42] Mrs. Thin Elk thanked them and said, 'That is more than enough for curing my own granddaughter.' You see, old man Thin Elk was Dad's brother. He, too, had been a powerful medicine man.

"He had told people that when he died his body should be thrown into the White River, and he would come back to life, but they didn't do that because it was winter when he died, and the river was frozen. And that is how I got well and finally went to school when I was ten.

"So you see, Donna, I never got the chance to go to school when I was little. The fall of 1910 I was to start school, but by then I had changed my mind. I would soon be eleven years old, and I was too embarrassed to be in kindergarten. Besides, I was the youngest girl, and my dad was getting old and didn't want me to go to school.

"That fall a man came to the house. He called Dad outside. He and Dad argued in Indian, back and forth. Soon my brother George came into the cabin and said, 'Dad and that man are arguing about you. That man says if Mom and Dad don't send you to school in Pierre, the Indian police will come and arrest them.'[43]

"My brother looked scared. 'I don't want them to arrest Mom and Dad, but I don't want you to go to school, either. I want you to stay with us, little sister, like you always have,' he said.

"When I got to school, I didn't like it at all because I was so lonely; and I was too big, compared to the other children in my class. We worked at chores like gardening, sewing, or laundry half the day and took classes in the afternoon.[44] Eventually, I got to really like school. I never got tired of learning, Donna, but I never even got to finish the eighth grade. I was sixteen, and that was the summer I married your dad. I always wished I could have gotten

more education, but I started too late. You have the chance
to start early and go as far as you want. I don't want you to
leave, but if I keep you home the police will come and you
don't want that, do you?"

"No!" I said.

                                Lucy Marries

EVEN AFTER WHAT Mom told me about school, I was still
afraid to be going so far from home; I didn't want Mom to
be sad. I asked her, "How did you meet Dad? At school?"

"Yes, it was at school, but your dad was not a student. He had already finished school long before that. He
had moved back to the reservation and married a woman
named Mattie High Dog. She died, so your father was at
home alone.

"One of my friends sent a letter that spring to a male
cousin of hers. She told him she had found the perfect wife
for him. She told me that she had the perfect husband for
me. She said, His name is James Hart Swan. He has been
to school in Chilocco, Oklahoma, and he even has two
years past high school at Lawrence, Kansas. He is very educated and very handsome and comes from a good family.
His father was a chief.'

"One day my friend ran over to where I was working.
'He's coming! He's coming!' she yelled.

'Who?' I asked.

'My cousin, James. He's coming to meet you. If you're
right for him, he wants to marry you!' 'Marry me! Oh, no,
I thought. I'm just a little girl!'

"Why, just last summer I spent most of my time riding
from powwow to powwow on the reservation with my sister, I told her. Oh, what fun we had, though. We stayed
with older relatives. Whenever we needed money, I took a
tooth off the elk's tooth dress Mom let me use. I would sell

the tooth and then we would have money. It still makes
me laugh, Donna, when I think about how angry your
Grandma got when she saw the dress![45]

"Still I told my friend, 'I am too young; this man will
never want to marry me.'

"Well, he came, and he was handsome, and so old, I
thought. He asked me if I could sew. 'Yes,' I said.

'Can you cook?'

'Yes, I can.'

'Do you know how to hitch a team?'

'Yes. I can do beadwork, and make moccasins, and . . .'

'Never mind all that!' he said. 'If you marry me, you
won't have to worry about any of that!'

'But I'm just so dumb. I'm only a sixth grader,' I
told him.

'That's okay. You don't have to be educated; if you can
read and figure and speak English, that's plenty,' he said.[46]

"Soon he left. I never heard from him until I got a letter from my brother. He said James had gone to Rosebud,
to White River, and spoke to him about me. In the letter
he said, 'This man has no wife; he has gone to high school,
and even beyond that! He seems like a good man, and I
am sure he can take care of you.'

"Mom didn't like the idea at all. Still, my brother was
the man of the family, now that my dad was gone, and he
said to marry this man.[47] My friend helped me make a wed-
ding dress, and many presents for me, even for a baby!
They teased me so much; we would just laugh, imagining
what it would be like to be married. About two weeks after
the letter came, James came to the school with my brother
George, and we drove to White River. We were married
there, stayed a few days with my mother, then moved to
Cherry Creek.

"So you see, I was young, too young. I want you to go
to Immaculate Conception Mission and learn all you can.
I want you to finish high school and be a nurse or something that you want—something so you could make your

own way in this world with your brains and education. That is what your father wants for you also. I know when you leave for school you will be lonely; so will I. We will all miss you very much, but we will have the summers together, and we will visit you as often as we can. So when you go to school, pay attention, learn all you can."

I didn't really feel any better about leaving home, but if this was what Mom and Dad both wanted, I thought, "I will go along with it and try not to be sad."

  Buffalo Hunt: 1933

So, THAT JANUARY I went to Immaculate Conception School in Stephan. I was so lonely at first I would just cry myself to sleep. I wanted to go home so bad! Finally, it was time to go home for the summer; I was so happy to be going home. The summer of 1935 I was seven years old. We used to go to Grandma Julia's home on the White River every summer for a week or so, to pick uta [acorns]. It seemed like they were plentiful over there. They don't grow at all near Cherry Creek.

All summer long in Cherry Creek we picked plums and cherries and different kinds of berries. Only the women would go. We sure had fun doing that. Grandma, Mom, or one of the older ladies along would tell us a story while we were resting or having lunch.

This time we were collecting acorns. Grandma would roast them; then we'd crack them open and take the little nut inside, out. She would pound them into a fine powder like corn meal. Grandma used a stone mortar and pestle and a rawhide bowl to catch the powder. We would take turns helping her, because it was hard work. We were always happy when we did that. Grandma would make wojapi [pudding] out of the first ones she pounded. It tasted real good.

Immaculate Conception Mission, Stephan, South Dakota, 1938.

We were doing that, watching Grandma pound acorns, and Mom said, "I'll tell you about our buffalo hunt last summer." She had already told me that story, but I really liked it. When Mom would tell it, her eyes would dance, and she would laugh and smile and sort of act it out. So she started.

"Your Uncle Dick Swan came by the place one day, and he was really smiling about something. He said, 'Get that old man of yours out here; I want to talk to him about something.' So I called your father. When he came out to the yard, your uncle Dick said, 'I've heard something I thought I would tell you. Well, you know how you tease me about being a no good BIA boss farmer? Well, this time I think you'll change your story. We got a letter from a Mr. Phillips, who has a ranch north of Pierre.'

"Dad interrupted and said, 'Do you mean the one that has that big herd of buffalo?'

'You're pretty darn smart, then, aren't you?' Dick teased. 'Well, anyway, they've been hurt very bad by the drought down there, even worse than here! Well, he sold his herd of buffalo to the state because he couldn't feed them anymore, and they were getting sick. They drove them over to the Black Hills to that Custer State Park.'

'So!' Dad said.

'So, they lost some strays on the way, and he said anyone from Cheyenne River Reservation was welcome to go hunt for them, kill them, and take the meat and hides home!' Dick said.

"Your dad stood there, smiling. I think that old man of mine was really surprised. 'So, what do you think?' Dick asked.

'I think we should keep it kind of quiet and go hunt for them,' your dad said. Then I got excited. It sounded like it would be exciting to do that.

"I had Orby on my breast then, so I had to take him. Do you remember when we left for a week last summer? Well, that's the time we went to hunt for them. Grandma, here, said she would stay with you girls, so we went.

"We spent a day packing. About nine families came with us. They were your uncles, Yellow Owls, old man Horn, and from Red Scaffold Lone Eagles and the Knife families.[48] We left early so we could get towards Pierre before we camped that night. Everybody was joking and laughing, and really excited. Uncle Dick said that they were last seen someplace north of Pierre, and that was all he knew. So we pitched camp and made a fire. Everybody just kept visiting and laughing until very late.

"Early, about dawn, the men went out. We were near some broken country. The old men along said this would be a good place to hunt for them. Some of the men took lances, others took bows, and some, like your dad, took their rifles along. I went with some of the women in a wagon. We were going to help butcher and haul the meat. The first day towards dusk the men said they saw tracks but no animals.

In camp that night, everybody talked about how we could find them—the old folks knew where to look.[49] We talked about how many buffalo were out there. That next day we left early again. We had gone a long way towards the southeast, and pretty soon they saw one. They got really excited, especially the old men who lived before the reservations.

"The men took their shirts off, and two old men, old man Horn and Knife, made battle cries, took their lances, and charged the buffalo. It was a young bull, and they really had to chase it. Those men acted like they were young again. Pretty soon they closed, and old man Horn pushed his lance into the side of that bull. So did old man Knife. Soon the animal went down. The men really cheered, and we made waiaglata (a trill)! Uncle Dick finished the bull off with his rifle.[50]

"We loaded the buffalo onto the wagon, then headed back to camp. We butchered it and divided the meat. We kept everything, jerking all the meat and insides, and put it on drying racks in the sun. The next day we did the same thing. Your Aunt Nancy would say every morning, 'Bring back everything, even the hooves!' I teased her and said, 'You can have the hooves.' So she really laughed.

"The next day we got two buffalo, a cow and a calf, and we hauled them back. Everything was butchered up in an hour. The men were really teasing us. Well, it went on that way; we got eleven all together. Every day it was exciting; different men took turns. One old man got one with a bow and arrow! The men would make war whoops, and we'd make a cry, le, le, le, le! Each family got a whole buffalo. It was nice to do that, go on a buffalo hunt."

Grandma said, "It was good for you to do that, daughter. When I was a little girl, there were many buffalo, and we hunted them all summer and jerked and dried the meat. I'm glad you got to try that." Grandma just sat there smiling, her hand up to her face.[51] "I wish I could have seen it," she said.

Mom's story was over, and they went on pounding uta. I went in the shade and took a nap, I think. When I woke up, Mom said, "We should have enough acorns by tomorrow. Then we will head back towards Cherry Creek."

Mice People

THE SUMMERS WHEN I was small were the happy times. We spent many hours playing with toys. We didn't have toys like children have today. We had very few "white man's" toys; we made most of our toys. Our Grandma made us beaded buckskin dolls. They had beaded leggings and moccasins, and the dresses were fully beaded. She made some with shell dresses with the little shells that look like elk's teeth. When we were smaller, she made us replicas of the fancy dolls. These were cloth. We had little blankets for our dolls and made tents out of full-sized blankets.

When I was a little older, Grandma bought us a little wood stove and made us a small wall tent. In the warm morning sun we would go out from the house, usually near the creek, and play moving from place to place. We would set up our little village, take it down, and move it again.

One day, we played that morning till early afternoon. Manuel called to us from a hill to go home for dinner. As I walked up the creek bank, my foot broke through the ground. When I pulled my foot out I saw four small mice in a nest. Orby picked up a mouse and started chasing Shirley and I. I wasn't really scared, but Orby was really enjoying himself, so I just ran and ran. I was always a fast runner.

When we got back to the house, Orby still had the mouse. Mom came out into the bright sun and, as she squinted her eyes, asked Orby why he had that mouse. "Do you know that mice should never be tortured? Sometimes they help people. I'll tell you a true story about mice (intunkala), and how they helped your Grandmother High Pine.[52]

"When Manuel was about four months old, Rosie Iyotte was living with Grandma. My sister Sarah was living with the babies' dad. Sarah never went home; she was too busy spending some money she had gotten from a land sale. We heard this was going on, so I was worried about Grandma. Dad said, 'We'll go over there in December and make sure your mother has firewood and food.'

"It was very cold when we started out for White River. We brought a four-horse team just in case we hit a storm and got stuck. We also brought a saddle horse. The trip took us two days. The first night we stopped near Stanford, South Dakota.

"We got to White River towards evening. No smoke was coming from Mom's cabin. Dad looked at me and told me to go see if anyone was home. I looked inside and found the house cold and dark. There was a window on the north side of the cabin. From the dim light, I could barely see what looked like a person with blankets over their head, lying on Grandma's cot.

"When I found Grandma, I yelled to your dad, 'Come quick! Ina! Ina!' I called, yet no noise came out. Dad lit a lamp, and from the light I could see Grandma's eyes were glazed, and she was very thin. There was the sound of a baby's cry from underneath Grandma's covers.[53]

'I'll get some wood and start a fire, you get some food cooked, and we'll see what we can do for your mom and Rosie,' Dad yelled from the yard.

"We fed her and made the baby milk. Soon Grandma was able to talk. She said, 'I was sitting here like this for four days. We were out of food and split wood and nobody came by. I was getting very cold so I started to pray for help. Mice were crawling on me and sort of nibbling on us. I prayed to those mice. Grandmother mouse, please send help and please don't crawl on us. And then I would sleep for a while, wake up, and sleep again. I got too weak to move so I just stayed here and waited for help to come. Then you came! I believe a mouse whispered to you and told you.'[54]

"Then Grandma went back to sleep. She woke the next morning; by then we had the house clean and warm. She smiled at me as she woke and said, 'Tell your husband to take that check from the drawer over to the store in White

River and buy some food for the baby and bring a bag of peanuts. I want to make an offering to the mice people.'[55] So that is what we did.

"So you see, children, the mice have a purpose here." Mom went on, "Everything on this earth has a purpose, the ants, badger, deer, even the flies! Everything but zuzeca [snakes]!", she said, laughing. "As far as I know they are good for nothing! So you should treat animals kindly and don't kill them for no good reasons!" she said, grinning at us. Then she said, "Sometimes when you are in trouble or can't get a horse to move, talk to it in a kind and respectful manner, and it will listen."

Robert Blue Hair's Mother

THE SIOUX HAVE many medicine people who use herbs, songs, and the pipe to doctor the sick. My grandfathers, Thin Elk and Runs Above, were medicine men like this. They cured sicknesses and helped many people.

When I was eight years old, we went to the Fourth of July in Faith. My dad was going to take us to the rodeo—a real rodeo! We were all excited, but that time I had a real bad tooth ache, and I was really suffering with it. Dad had a car then, and I was lying in the back seat.

I was too sick to go to the rodeo, and I was disappointed. I just cried. There was a woman from Cherry Creek who was a good herb doctor. Her name was Mrs. Blue Hair, and she was a real old-fashioned Indian woman. Mom saw Mrs. Blue Hair and her family camped not too far from us at the Faith fair. Mom went to talk to Mrs. Blue Hair about my toothache. "Yes, I can help her, at least until she has it pulled or fixed. Lay her down on the cot in your wall tent then pull the flaps down. I'll be over in a minute."

Soon Mom told me to get in the tent and pull the flaps down. "Why? What for?" I asked.

"She is going to try and doctor that tooth so you can go the rodeo," Mom said. Mrs. Blue Hair came. First she sang and prayed in Indian with her hands outstretched to each direction. When she had finished the medicine song, she bent over me. She sounded like a bear was in her chest. Mrs. Blue Hair took some white powdered medicine from a little buckskin sack and rubbed it all over my tooth. It looked like chalk. When she was finished, it hurt less. By the time the rodeo was ready to begin, my tooth was much better.[56]

              Thin Elk's First Fast

IT WAS SNOWING hard, and the wind howled and shook the windows. The winter of 1937 was a cold one. Dad had taken Shirley and I home from school for Christmas. In those days we had no television or radio. We did a lot of things like quilt or crochet or sew. Mom would spend as much time with us as she could. Grandma High Pine told us one time that Mom got so sad when we left for school in the fall, just seeing our clothes would sometimes make her cry. I always remembered her telling me this when I would feel lonely for Mom.

We finished eating one evening, Mom was tired, so I volunteered Shirley and I to clean up the dinner dishes if she would tell us a story from when she was young, or stories about our relatives. This evening Mom got a twinkle in her eye. "I'll tell you a story you haven't heard before," she said. So she started.

"The weather is very bad, and all that wind sounds scary. Well, I'll tell you a story about Grandpa Thin Elk and the time he was frightened by the weather. My father had three brothers. In those times everyone had their own name. Their names were Runs Above, Swift Bear, and Thin Elk. Runs Above was a well known doctor, a holy man. He had fasted many days for what he knew. Many people went to him for help with sickness and problems. Because of this, he had many horses and was well liked.[57]

"Runs Above and High Pine, your grandpa, were quite a bit older than Thin Elk. His mother was Pretty Shell Woman, middle wife of my grandfather. Thin Elk had a hard time at everything; people did not think much of him. The time came when Thin Elk decided he would become a wicasa wakon (holy man), or pejuta wicasa (herb man).

"Thin Elk asked Runs Above and High Pine to put him on the hill to fast and pray for a helper.[58] Runs Above did not think this was a very good idea, because Thin Elk was too young. He tried to talk him out of it. He told Thin Elk how serious a thing it was to fast, how it might be dangerous, and how difficult it would be to get a helper. Thin Elk teased them, saying, 'If Runs Above could do it, so could I.'

"Runs Above and my father started to get Thin Elk ready to go on the hill. They taught him many things about the creation, and how we came to be here, and how to pray with the pipe.[59] When it was nearing the time for Thin Elk to go on the hill, Runs Above instructed him not to leave the hill no matter what happens, to be brave, and to keep praying. They took Thin Elk to a high butte not far from the village. They placed white sage under a buffalo robe that Thin Elk would stand on. Then they put four small poles in the ground, one in each of the four directions. Next, they pierced Thin Elk, twice on his chest and twice on his back. They put wooden skewers through the slits and tied them with a strong sinew cord to each of the posts.[60]

"Last, they handed him his pipe and told him to pray, to be brave, and not to be frightened by anyone or anything. Then they left him there on that hill. About midnight there was a thunder and lightning storm. Soon Thin Elk came crashing back into camp. The dogs howled at him so loud that it woke the camp up. Those poles were bumping and dragging behind him, still fastened to his chest and back, and he was all muddy from falling.

"As Dad and my uncle unhooked Thin Elk from his
poles, they spoke to him, telling him that he should not
have left the hill. They told him that he should not have
gone on that fast unless he intended to go through with it.
Thin Elk was embarrassed now; people laughed at him,
but he did not give up. When he was a little older, he did
fast again and became a doctor. He helped many people
and came to be a well-respected man. I remember that
from when I was a little girl. So you see, when things are
hard for us, we are being tested. We have to overcome
the difficulty and go on, no matter how hard it seems
right then."

I didn't know it then, but the story about Thin Elk would
come back to me time and again in the years to come.

                              Horse Grandchildren

DAD WAS NOT home much of the time. It is a good thing
that Mom was an independent and resourceful person.
Grandma and Grandpa High Pine had done a good job
with Mom, preparing her for motherhood and life.

I remember early one summer, when I was about ten,
it was 1938. An elderly person Mom thought highly of had
passed away. She was being waked in a small church about
twenty-five miles from Cherry Creek. Mom wanted to pay
her last respects and help with the butchering and cooking
for the feast that always follows the funeral and burial.[61] It
had rained for two days, and puddles stood everywhere on
the gumbo. Mom said, "It will be muddy! I hope we don't
get stuck. We'll take the best team and the newer wagon
that Grandpa gave us.

"Madonna, go tell Ida One Feather to gather her kids
and anything she wants to bring, so we can pack the wagon
box." So I did. I ran all the way. Mrs. One Feather was a
friend of Mom's, and she had two boys and a little girl to
take with her.

We were finished loading and hitching the team to the wagon about 11:00 in the morning. The sun had disappeared behind dark clouds, and it looked threatening. "Come, let's get started," Mom called out. There were six of us all together, and our clothes, tents, and cooking supplies, so the wagon was quite heavy. We made deep ruts in the soft clay as we started for the wake.

About six miles from Cherry Creek there was a low place near the Cheyenne River that looked muddy, even from a distance. We were only a few yards into that place when we got stuck. Cornelius One Feather, Ida's oldest boy, asked Mom, "Should I get out and give the horses a slap so we can get going again?" "No, I'll do it," Mom said.

Mom reached under the seat and took out some oats and some rags. We all watched. She was smiling and sort of laughing out loud as she tied the rags around her shoes. She climbed down off the wagon and sank in wet gumbo clay up to her ankles. She could barely move as she struggled to get nearer the horses. She gave each of the horses a handful of oats and stroked their heads. She said, "Takoja unsilakano unpi yapi omani le elunkiiyapi na aka ehunpi woaste un komanipi ca. (Grandsons, help us! Help us that we will get out of this swamp and mud and take us to safety to where we are going. We are going for a good purpose)." She didn't get angry; she talked to them like they were people.[62] She never got angry or cursed. She just spoke very gently to them and rubbed their faces. Mom gave a gentle tug, and the horses strained to pull the wagon. It budged with a jolt and started to move.

Every time we got stuck, Mom would climb down with her gumbo-covered feet and talk with the horses. It took a while, but finally we made higher, drier ground. Mom climbed down and thanked the horses. Then she put her hands on her hips and pretended to do a little dance. We all howled with laughter. Finally, Mom couldn't hold it back anymore, and she started laughing so hard she couldn't continue her dance. Those gumbo clods were about a foot thick, and they made her feet look huge.

Late that day we got to the church. Mom had taken us over a rough road with no man. That's the kind of Mom she was. Nothing seemed to scare her. She faced life head on, often by herself.

❧   *The Flood*

WE WERE CAMPED at White River at Grandma High Pine's place gathering berries and acorns. Grandma was always in a good mood when we camped at her place. She would show us off to her neighbors and our relatives who lived near White River. We would stay up late at night, sitting near the fire, and she would tell us stories.

One night she stuck her head in the wall tent and asked if anyone would like a story. She would tease us this way and just smile. Nobody said anything. We just giggled and pulled our light blankets around our shoulders. Grandma lit the kerosene lamp suspended from the ridge pole. "Grandchildren, I will tell you a story, something that happened in my life when I was about your age. I was about seven years old then.

"We were free then, the year before the signing of the papers at Fort Laramie that fenced us in.[63] It was the moon of the popping trees, and we were trying to reach relatives that were said to be starving to the south.[64] The cold wind had chilled the horses, and many of the older people gathered to decide if the camp should be made in that place. The people decided to push on and reach a sheltered place along the Grey Waters River.[65]

"As the day went along, the sun came out, and the wind stopped. When we reached a sheltered place made by the steep walls of a ravine and cottonwood trees, we decided to camp. It was warm enough that the children were able to run and play without their winter robes. While we played, the older people set up camp.

"There was a man in our camp named Comes At First

Light. He had gotten his name when he was young man. He had returned from the west with a string of fat Crow ponies at the first light of day. He was a relation to my mother, but not close. Light was always making guesses about the future. Usually, they did not come true, but sometimes they would. He would get his signs in dreams while he slept.[66]

"On this day, Light, as he was called, made one of his predictions. He said, 'I have seen a Lakota camp in a flood of rushing waters. There was no sounds of screaming coming from the lodges. Perhaps this was our camp! We should camp further away from the river's edge.'

"In each family group there was a great discussion about what Light had been saying. By now everyone had heard of his dream and his prediction. Light and his family moved away from the main camp and began to set up their lodges among the cottonwood trees on a hillside not far from our camp.

"Mother and Father and some close relations were discussing Light's ability or lack of ability to tell the future. There was much laughing and joking. Finally, my father said we would move our tipi. As we prepared to move, Father teased Mother, making her laugh. He pretended not to know why she wished to camp so close to her male cousin. Some of the men grumbled that in the moon of the popping trees, it does not flood. 'It has been far too cold, and the ice on the river too thick for such a thing,' they said. Gradually almost half the camp moved up the old river bank to where our families had camped. Still, there was much teasing and joking directed towards us and among us, concerning the prophecy of old man Comes At First Light.

"About an hour before the sun came up, my mother yelled for us to get up and run out of the lodge. She didn't need to yell very loud, because we were covered with water and chunks of ice! We grabbed what we could and ran. When we came out of the lodge, other families were running through the ankle deep water up to a dry spot. It was still too dark to tell much, but the river was right next to us, and we could see some lodges that were collapsing.

"Soon the women had fires going for the children and old people. The men were wading into the icy water and pulled dogs, bundles, lodge covers, and people out of the water.

"As the black night changed to grey dawn, we saw a terrible thing. Only those lodges that camped on higher ground remained. Almost half our lodges were gone! In the river we could see drowned people, horses, dogs, even buffalo. All of the belongings of many who had survived were gone or floating away, and to make matters worse it had turned cold. I think at seven summers I was too young to realize how terrible this really was![67]

"The men and women cut their hair and slashed their arms; then a terrible keening went up among us that remained alive. The flood had come swiftly, so swiftly that there had not even been any screams from the lower camp, only the crashing of lodge poles, water, and ice.

"Later that day some of the families brought horses to the lodge of Comes At First Light. After that, when the old man made predictions, people listened a little better, but still most of his predictions never came true!"[68]

"What a scary thing to happen," I said.

"Yes, child, it was. Many bad things happened back then. It was not as good as some people say, because I saw this with my own eyes!" she said, smiling as she bent to tuck us in.

                                                 Warts: 1938

I WAS NEVER a pretty child like my sister Shirley! I used to look in the mirror by the wash stand and wish I was prettier.[69] To make things even worse, when I was about eleven or twelve, I got the worst case of warts! They had started on my hands, and soon they were on my face. I had a huge one on my nose, another on my chin, and they were all over my hands. I was so embarrassed! "How can I go back to school looking like this?" I cried to Mom and Grandma. "The kids will make fun of me, and I'll just die, I thought.

One day, Dad came up to me, he said, "It's time to get rid of your warts."

"Oh, do you really think I can?" I asked him.

"Sure! You go get a stick and sharpen a point on one end. Then find me the biggest potato you can." So when I fetched those things, I met Dad. He took me by the hand; then we walked southeast to the top of a little hill not far from the house. Dad stopped and prayed to each of the four directions. He prayed that the Grandfathers take my warts away. And he prayed that this was the right thing to do, because it was for his daughter.[70]

Next, he took out his pocket knife, handed it to me, and said, "Cut the potato in half and rub the cut side all over your warts. The one on your nose, too." He reminded me. "Now, put both halves back together exactly as they were cut. Now, push that sharp stick through both halves; next, face north with me, throw the potato over your shoulder, and don't look back!" When I had done that, Dad smiled at me, took my hand, and we walked back towards the house.

I didn't know whether Dad's remedy would work or not. I never gave it much thought. A few days before we were to leave for school, Mom gave me a new dress she had just finished sewing. "Here, put this on; you will really look pretty," she said in a soft voice.

As I adjusted the collar, I could see my hands in the mirror. They looked different. Yes, of course! "The warts are gone," I screamed out loud. I looked at the ones on my face. "The ones on my face are gone, too!" Mom ran and hugged me. I was so happy. Now the kids at school wouldn't have anything to tease me about. I looked forward to school now, like I did every year.

After that Mom sometimes would tease Dad. She would tell Manuel, "Go fetch that medicine man to dinner."

Then, grinning, she would serve Dad first, saying, "I'd better feed that holy man wart doctor, before he gives me warts!"

                                    Family Troubles: 1940

AFTER I WAS grown and on my own, my mother told me a lot about what happened to her in her life. She told me about the mistreatment she got on account of us kids. I was never aware of the problems my parents had when I was a child; I hardly remember hearing them argue. I do remember one time in particular, though. My father was the one who bought everything. He wouldn't even let us pick out our own clothes. We were going back to Stephan; it was 1939 or 1940.

Manuel and Kermit were going to the Old Agency school; it was the year Manuel was to graduate from high school. The boys had made it known for some time that they wanted cowboy boots. Grandma High Pine told the boys not to worry: "If your dad won't buy some western boots, I'll bring you back some when I come from White River next spring." It was easy for us girls because we always wore a dress and oxford shoes at the mission.

Dad overheard the conversation with Grandma and told us angrily, "I buy the clothes, and they will wear what I buy!" Then he turned toward the yard, slamming the door behind him. Soon after that he went to shop in Faith. Late that night he came back and started to unload the wagon. The boys ran outdoors to help bring the boxes inside.

Kermit said to Manuel, "Let's see what kind of shoes that old man brought us."

Before they could even get in the boxes, Dad yelled angrily, "Well, you don't like them shoes? Well, as long as you live under this roof, you'll wear what I buy! And I'll buy what I like!"

Mom was looking through those clothes, searching through the boxes. I could tell she was angry with Dad; still, she didn't say anything. Dad grabbed Mom by the arm and kind of jerked her around. He told us all to go to bed. We ran off in a hurry. We were scared by the way he had jerked Mom's arm.

The next morning Grandma was sitting way off from the house. The boys were already up and gone for the morning. "Grandma, why are you sitting way over here?" we asked.

"Oh, I just wanted to sit here for a while," she answered quietly. We knew she had been crying, so we sat with her for a while. Finally, we left her there and went back to the house.

Uncle Dick brought Mom back from the store in Cherry Creek about noon. We noticed a bruise under Mom's eye.[71] It was kind of quiet all that day. Late in the day Kermit rode his horse up to the house and said to me, "Cicila, [little sister] I'm going to Uncle Frank's and speak with him; Manuel is in Cherry Creek. He's going to stay there for a while. Stay away from the old man, if he comes back, and watch out for Mom and Grandma." Then he rode off.

That night Uncle Frank Council Bear came back with Kermit. Manuel had come back earlier from Cherry Creek. We were all sitting at supper, except Dad. My uncle broke the silence and said, "Every family encounters these problems. People part, and either the man or the woman takes the kids, but it never works out for the kids. You should stay here, together. This is a good family. You are a good Catholic woman," he said turning towards Mom. "You should try to stay here and patch things up."

Grandma was starting to cry. She said, "I don't like what James said and did to my daughter. He has no right to treat her that way. My daughter and I are going back to White River, and the younger ones and any of the older children are welcome to come with us."

Kermit said, "I don't want you and Mom to go! This is our house—we built it. This is our land. The one who has

to leave is Dad! You just stay here." I looked at Kermit, so
proud of the kind of man he was growing up to be.

It took a few days for things to calm down and get back
to normal. Dad finally came home a few days later and
took Shirley and I back to Stephan. Years later Mom told
me that there were other times that she had been hit. It
made me feel very sad.

Ishna Ti Cha Lowan—Becoming a Woman

AMONG THE LAKOTA people, we have a way of marking a
ceremony for young women when they have their first
moon, or monthly cycle.[72] The day that I got my first
moon, we were living outside Cherry Creek. Mom and
Grandma closed off a little space for me to stay with ropes
and blankets.[73] I moved in Grandma's little cabin, and that
is where Grandma said I must stay for the next four days
and four nights.

Grandma Julia instructed me not to look out the windows. I was not to stand at the door and peek out or let my
thoughts go outside that little enclosure. She said, "You are
to stay busy doing something all the time; if you are not
cooking, washing, or cleaning the house you should be
sewing or beading. Whatever you do, if you are sewing and
you make a mistake, you should not rip it out. If you do,
you will be that way the rest of your life. If you do rip it
out, it will be your habit in all things during your life time.
So just keep going and the next time do it better," she
instructed.

I didn't have to try very hard, because Mom or Grandma
were there to remind me and show me the right way to do
things the whole time. I made a doll with a cloth Indian
dress, beaded moccasins, and leggings. I had never done
beadwork before. I sewed buttons on all my dad's and
brother's shirts. I sewed all my mom's old dresses. I sewed
up and patched up bib overalls. Then Grandma Julia cut

some quilt blocks, and I made them up into two quilt tops. She taught me how to cook in the old ways that her mother had taught her.

Grandma told me, "Within these days you are not to have a bad disposition or think bad thoughts about anyone or anything. Try to be happy and not to get angry or else that will also be your way in life." She told me not to scratch my head or itch myself anywhere for these four days. Grandma had made me a stick; I had to clean my nails or scratch with that stick.

Every day she prayed over me, but before she would pray, Mom and Grandma would bathe me in water in which they added sage and green cedar.[74] Then Grandma High Pine would pray, "Grandfathers above and in the four directions, make Madonna a good woman. Help her to treat guests with hospitality. Grandfathers, help her to be a good worker. Grandfathers, and Maka Ina (Mother Earth), help Madonna to be a good mother. I pray that the food she cooks in her life will be good for those that eat it. Grandfathers, help her to be a good wife and live with the same man all her life. Grandfathers, bless her with healthy children." These are the kinds of things she asked of the Tunkasilapi [Grandfathers].

During those special days Grandma would take me outside and teach me. She told me everything in life is sacred. She said, "You should never curse things out or say sicala [it's bad] or anything like that. Those things, even if you don't like them, were created for a purpose. Everything is sacred. All the things you learn during these four days are important. These teachings will help you for a lifetime. You should try to learn all you can so that when you take a husband, you can do all these things."

In these four days, as in the past, Grandma instructed me in many things. She would teach me things by reminding, "We should always thank Wakon Tonka for all that he has given us, all that he has done for us. We should thank him for our health. You should never forget to pray to him when you are in trouble or in need of anything."

Unci [Grandma] also told me, "The Sun, Wi, is Wakon Tonka. We pray to him; we also call him Tunkasila, which means Grandfather. I have prayed with the peace pipe since I was a young woman and my father gave me a pipe." When Grandma prayed, she held the mouthpiece pointed towards the sky to the Wi Tunkasilapi, Grandfather Sun; next, she held it to the four directions, Wiyahinjanpate, the East, Waziyata, the North, Wiyakysiyata, the West, and Itokala, the South, then to Maka Ina, our Mother Earth.

She would say, "The directions are also our friends; we pray to them in time of need or necessity. The earth is our grandmother, unci to us all, to all living things. Hanwi, the Moon, is also our friend, and Tate, the Wind, and Whope, the beautiful one. She was the Buffalo Woman, the white Buffalo Calf Maiden that brought us the sacred Calf Pipe.

"Wakinyan, the Thunder, is also your friend, and Tatonka, the Buffalo, and the Bear, Hu Nunpa, Tate Tob, the Four Winds, the whole universe—each spirit also represents something. The Tatonka Sicun (Buffalo Spirit), represents the energy of life as food and shelter for the Lakota people."

She also taught me about the Four Great Virtues which govern the conduct of the Lakota people. They are generosity, bravery, fortitude (long suffering or patience), and moral integrity.[75] She instructed me, "Watch out for iktomi [trickster or spider], they can appear as bad people or show themselves in other tricky ways. Some deer can transform themselves into people. If you like a person or have a secret crush on someone, the deer people can know your thoughts and appear as that person and lead you astray. They can make your mind go crazy. You should be fearful and respectful of all these kind.

"There is a man for every woman; in time that man will come along. You won't even know each other. You will just meet one day and know this is the man for you." These are the kinds of things she told me and reminded me of during that four days.

At the end of the four days, I again went back into the regular world, but things were different now. About two days later they made a feast and invited everyone in Cherry Creek. Then they gave away what I had made and many things they had been making and put aside for this day. Grandma gave a talk about what had taken place, instructing other women to do the same with their daughters, so that they could have good lives. Then she prayed and fed all the visitors and gave them a gift of a shawl, a quilt, or food.

Many things were different for me after that. I was a young woman now. It was hard for my brothers to understand. I could no longer play with them like I used to. I used to climb trees, play ball, and all those sorts of things. Grandma had instructed me that I was not to play with the boys like I had before, after I came out. I couldn't run around, climb trees, or play with my brothers anymore.[76] I was thirteen years old then.

Grandmother believed in Christianity; she was baptized a Catholic. Shortly after that time, she was picking berries with us. We asked, as we had many times in the past, why she prayed with the pipe. She told us, "It is the same as the Christian way. All prayers are good! You could have a pipe and pray with it if you want; the creator will still listen."

Grandma Julia would sometimes go to church and receive communion, but every day, every morning and night, she would pray with her pipe for all of us.

 Rummage Clothes

1942 WAS THE first time we ever heard of rummage clothes. The Catholic priest, Father Manning, brought a pickup load of used rummage clothes. He stopped by our house and asked Mom and Maggie Creek, "Why don't we have a sale and sell these rummage clothes? We could donate the proceeds to the church!" The ladies thought this was a good idea, so they helped Father unload the clothes at the Catholic meeting hall.

The little log cabin meeting hall was just filled with oodles of clothing, shoes, everything! Almost everyone in Cherry Creek went over to the meeting house for the sale. People were really going through those clothes, buying blouses, jackets, dresses, and shoes. Mom got right in there and picked out some dresses for Shirley and I.

We took our "new" clothes home, and Mom washed them for us. We ironed them and tried them on so Mom could alter them if they needed it. My brothers were still in school then, so we were getting ready to go back to school that fall. Mom said, "You girls better pack your suitcases—pack your dresses and your undershirts, too." Shirley and I started packing our "new" dresses into our bags. We counted how many each of us had, and here I had seventeen dresses, and Shirley had fifteen.

We were eating supper that evening, and Shirley said, "Mom, Madonna has seventeen dresses and me, I only have fifteen!" We all laughed and laughed. After that my brother would keep teasing Shirley, saying "Make room for the girl with fifteen dresses!" Before that, we were lucky to have even three dresses. That was the first, but certainly not the last, we heard of rummage clothes.[77]

   Grandma High Pine's Death: 1943

IN 1942 WE SPENT our last summer with Grandma. Every spring when school ended, we knew we would soon have her with us again. She was a genuine good person, and she was always telling us of the good things in life. She prayed every evening with her pipe, and then she would help us pray in our way.

One day after doing the evening dishes, Shirley and I went out to sit in the evening sun. When we rounded the corner of the house, Grandma was finishing her prayers. She saw us and, smiling, waved her hand for us to come over and visit with her. She rubbed our backs and said, "I wish you never had to grow up. You will have to face many difficult and painful things in your life. When you grow up and have children, it will be painful. I wish it was not that way, but that is the way it is."

She kind of told us the facts of life. She told us, "You don't have to go out and look for a man or a boyfriend. Keep to yourselves, be quiet, and be a lady. The good men will find you. Don't chase boys; the girls who do that, end up in trouble. You should listen to your mom and dad. They know much more than you."

And as she had many times in our lives, she reminded us, "Don't ever steal, tell lies, or hurt anyone in your hearts or minds or deeds."

It seemed to me that Grandma knew so much more than anyone else. She told us traditional stories and things that had happened to her in her long, hard life. Yet she only knew two words in English, yes and no. She had to sign her checks by putting her thumb print on them.

Grandma Julia had a skin disease that made her skin lose its color and turn white.[78] The doctor had told Mom that when those remaining brown spots turned white, she would die. So I sat there listening to her advice and looking at those brown spots. She still had big brown spots on her cheeks and chin. We used to really watch those spots and worry about her.

"You'll be going back to school soon, and I'll be going back to White River a few days after that. Don't worry about me," she said, wiping the tears from our eyes. As we sobbed and hugged her, she said, "I'll come back in the spring. By then your brother Kermit will be back from the war, and I want to see him. I want to live until both of your brothers are back from the war."

Her talk of living until spring made me feel sad and worried. I guess she was trying to tell us she couldn't live forever. We never would have guessed, as we held her in

Julia Brave Eagle High Pine in 1941, shortly before her death.

the warm sun, that this would be the last summer we would have her.

Mom and Dad came after us at the Mission on May 6, 1943, forty-three days after Grandma had died. I always resented Dad for that. Other kids got to go home for funerals, but we never did. Mom resented it, too, and although she didn't speak of it until years later, things like this hurt her feelings and made her resent Dad.

Dad met us at the school grounds and said, "We're going to White River for a few days, then go home to Cherry Creek." That was all he said, so we didn't think anything of it, although Mom was awful quiet. It took us a whole day to get there. As we came over the last hill, we would see Grandma's house. She lived about seven miles out in the country from the town of White River, and it was dusk when we got there.

We could see our aunt coming toward the gate. She was all dressed in black. Aunt Mary called in a shaky voice, "Your grandma isn't here anymore, she is gone." We got out of the wagon and ran to her house. There was nothing in Grandma's house![79] We couldn't believe that Dad had not said anything to us about it.

The little cemetery was across the river and up the hill from the house. We just kept running all the way to the cemetery. There were fresh flowers on Grandma's grave. We stood there crying very hard, not knowing what to say or do.

When Mom got to the grave, she had a strange and angry look on her face. She stood there quietly, and finally she could not hold back the tears. "Ina! Ina! (Mother, Mother)," she cried, over and over again wiping her eyes. We were all standing there not saying anything, and then we walked slowly back towards my aunt's house, back towards Grandma's empty house that had been the place of so many special times.

Finally, Mom spoke. Looking at Dad with anger in her eyes, she said, "There is no need for us to come back to White River anymore!"

Aunt Mary began to cry, and she said, "I'm still alive. I will try to take the place of Grandma. Please stay for a few days. I want you to visit me, because I feel sad and lonely for Mom, too. I still want to see you, Sister," she said, turning towards Mom. "I'll come to Cherry Creek to visit you like Grandma did."

So we did. We visited her, but in a few days we left for Cherry Creek. Aunt Mary was Mom's sister, and she kept her word. She was like a grandmother to us after that. Still, Mom never got over Grandma Julia's death and the fact that Dad had not let her attend her own mother's funeral.

🐾   *Prairie Fire at Immaculate Conception*

IN 1942, a prairie fire got started that almost burned down the mission. I think it got going first at Degray, South Dakota, about sixty miles northeast of the mission. The fire traveled a long distance, burning everything in its path.

That afternoon the fire came towards us. I was sewing with four other girls. We were in the little boys' sewing room, under their dorm. We were mending clothes for the little boys. Sister Cornelius was with us, and she said, "We are finished darning these socks. Madonna, would you run over to the laundry and get some more?"

I went over to the laundry, and here, when I got there, some girl said, "Did you know there is a big prairie fire coming, and it's headed straight for the mission? All of us high school girls have to go over to the gymnasium and get heavy clothes on and then go out and fight fire. Go back and look, if you don't believe us!" So I did go and look.

The laundry was on the second floor of the building, so I ran around to the back steps, and oh, it was bad! You could see the flames way up in the air. I told the girls with me, "I'm supposed to bring a load of socks over to Sister Cornelius."

"Oh, you won't need any socks after today," one of the

older girls said, laughing. "The mission will be burned down!"

"Well, I better take the socks anyway," I told them. I took two baskets of socks and ran all the way back down to the basement of the little boys' dorm. "Sister, Sister Cornelius!" I shouted. "There is a great big prairie fire coming, and we are supposed to run over to the gymnasium and get heavy clothes to fight fire!"

All the girls jumped up. "Oh, no! You all stay right here; I'll go and have a look," Sister said. She went upstairs and was soon back. She looked really upset and said, "Okay, you put your darning away just like normal, finish what you are doing, then clean the floor up and everything as usual."

So we did. We hurried and put everything away and were going to run out, when Sister said, "No, you come here and kneel down." Sister prayed over us, and she made us pray. Then she sprinkled us with holy water so we would be safe. When she got through, we all ran outside, around the northwest side of the building.

Sister Cornelius made us kneel down again, facing the fire, and we prayed again, "Dear Jesus, watch over us, and watch over the girls who are going to fight the fire, so that no harm will come to them. We pray that the fire will be put out and the mission saved." Then she sprinkled us with holy water again and said, "Now you can go, but just in case we don't see each other again," she gave each of us a hug, with tears in her eyes; she finished, "God love you, and God bless you."

When she let us go, we all ran over to the gymnasium. One of the Sisters said, "All those with little brothers and sisters are supposed to bring them to the little girls' playroom and get them ready. Get some food, enough for three days, and get clothing and blankets."

I had Shirley and Orby to take care of. I ran all the way over there with some of the other boys and girls that also had little ones to take care of. I got blankets, some food, and clothing. I handed them to Shirley and said, "No matter what happens, you just stay together; don't leave Orby for anything! Don't worry about me—I'll be alright. Orby, please don't cry." Then I left.

We ran back to the gymnasium, where they gave us heavy clothes, overalls, boots, and gunny sacks. They told us to tie our hair up so it wouldn't catch fire. We were loaded into trucks; then they took us to a field near a stock dam, about two hundred yards from the mission dairy barn. The fire was coming fast now! There was a cornfield on the west side of us and a small creek, on the east side that ran over towards the main buildings. This is where we started to fight fire.

It was really roaring loudly. Just when the fire reached the stock dam, it divided, one part racing around the west side of us; the other part jumped the creek and burned our cornfield and all the mission gardens. But it did not burn the mission!

About one hundred yards to the south there was a farm, and that is where the fire came back together. It burned the entire farm—cattle, pigs, chickens, the barns, the house, everything! We could hear the burning animals screaming, yet the mission was left, like an island of green in an ocean of black.

We started to move with the fire, further and further with the fire. We just kept wetting our gunny sacks and whipped the burning grass, trying to stop this terrible monster. I don't know how long we kept at it; we never stopped to even look up at the sky. We just kept going and going, moving with the fire. I was so tired! Three of us girls stuck together. One of them had a watch, so I asked her what time it was getting to be. She looked up and said, "Three o'clock in the morning!"

"Let's stop and find a truck where we can get some water to drink," one of the girls suggested. So we were just standing there; soon a truck came along. We were walking towards it when some other kids joined us. We walked over towards where the truck was and asked the driver for some water.

They gave it to us. Then the man that was driving said, "All you kids from the mission are supposed to gather over by that bus. They are going to take you back, now that the fire is under control."

"Where are we?" I asked.

"You're about seven miles southeast of Fort Thompson." "All that way," I thought. All that way we fought the fire! From Stephan, where the mission was, to Fort Thompson is seventeen miles, and we were seven miles further than that. We hadn't even known it, just wetting our gunny sacks and fighting fire, with no rest.

The girls and I went back to the bus and just sat there. Our faces were just as black as our hair, and our hair was burnt. We were a sight! We started to laugh at each other. You couldn't tell who was who. We sat there laughing until everyone was back. The driver asked that the younger ones go back first; then he came back for the rest of us.

When we got back to the mission, the sisters had food ready for us to eat. The priest who was superintendent of the school came into the mess hall and said, "There will be no school tomorrow or the next day. You don't have to worry about school tomorrow or the next day. You just eat, wash up, and go to bed. You can sleep as much as you want to. When you get hungry, just get up and eat."

But I couldn't sleep. I just kept remembering, thinking about all the farms I had seen burn up and the screaming of the animals. I kept coughing and coughing. Every time I wiped my mouth, black stuff was there. Finally, as the sun was coming up, I was coughing less, and I fell asleep.

                           School: 1943

I HAD LOST a lot of weight that summer, and when I saw Sister Cornelius, I asked her if I didn't look skinny to her. Sister said, "Maybe, but don't worry, you'll gain it back soon." I hadn't told her that I had pains in my chest and back. I was always catching cold, and when I would cough, black stuff would come up. I guessed it was still the smoke from the prairie fire. I tried not to think about it, and I put it in the back of my mind.

There were several other girls complaining of things like that. We had a girls' basketball team, and I played on it. It seemed like a few of the girls on the team would have those bad coughing spells like mine.

The first girl to get really sick was Ramona Jewett. She was playing on the swings one warm fall day, and someone was pushing her back and forth. Suddenly, she fell off the swing, landing hard on her back. She started bleeding from her mouth. They carried her back into the school and then to the infirmary. The Sisters said there was nothing wrong with her, so they let her go back to classes in a couple of days. She was playing kickball with some other little girls one day when she had another hemorrhage.

Several days later they told us Ramona had to be taken to the sanitorium because she was very sick. She died about two months later. The next one to get really sick was a girl named Seeking Land. She just started hemorrhaging one day, and before they could get her to the hospital in Fort Thompson, she was dead! Like they had with Ramona Jewett, they told us she died from quick consumption.[80]

I had a good friend named Rosie St. Pierre. She was from Turtle Mountain Reservation in North Dakota. She was tall, very pretty, and quite a basketball player. We were practicing one day when she jumped to catch a rebound. When she came down, she dropped the ball and grabbed hard at her chest. "Something popped in here!" she said, pointing to her ribs. Pretty soon blood started coming from her mouth. I was so scared! Not just for Rosie, but for all of us!

The sisters came quickly and took her over to the infirmary. Later they told us they had taken her over to St. Mary's in Pierre, about eight or nine that same night, by ambulance. Whenever anything important would happen,

Kathryn Grey Owl and Madonna Swan at Immaculate Conception
Boarding School, 1943.

the superintendent of the school would come over to the girls' recreation room. He came that evening and motioned with his hand for us to be quiet. In a shaky voice he said, "I'm sorry to tell you, but Rosie St. Pierre has passed away." His words went through me like a gunshot. No one said a word, we just stared at Father.

He continued, "Her parents are coming from Turtle Mountain, and they want to have a one night wake here in our chapel. Then they will take the body back for the burial at Turtle Mountain." So they did. When the body was ready, they brought it to the chapel. We went to the wake that night after she died. I looked at that wooden coffin.

Beautiful Rosie, so full of life; now she was dead. We didn't tell the sisters, but there were many more of us who feared that we would be the next to follow Rosie. We had the wake, and they took her home.

I had another good friend, and her name was Alvina Sargeant. I worried about her because her pains were worse than mine. After they took Rosie we were talking, and she said, "Do you suppose we have the same thing as Rosie?" There! Someone had said it, someone had asked that horrifying question. After that we used to talk more openly about it.

We would say, "Well, if it's going to happen, it will, and there is nothing much any of us can do about it." After that we kept a very close watch on each other.

There was a fifth grader named Rita His Chases. She was from Kennel, on Standing Rock.[81] Suddenly, one evening she started to hemorrhage. The farthest they got her was the infirmary. She was dead before they got her there! These things took place in the fall and early winter of 1943. There was a favorite sister. Her name was Sister Cordella. She was always frail looking. She was the first Sister to get sick with consumption. They took her to a hospital in Denver.

The next to get sick was Sister Andrew. She was younger and had fought fire with us, that time of the big fire. After that fire she had a funny voice. Sometimes she would lose her voice completely. Later they told us she had tuberculosis of the throat. TB, tuberculosis—there was that word I would hear so often and come to hate with my whole soul. All those deaths that had been called "quick consumption" were tuberculosis.

Kermit Comes Home: Spring 1943

MY BROTHER KERMIT was stationed in the South Pacific during World War II. He was wounded and shipped home in 1943. He had a bullet wound on the left side of his chest. He went through surgery in Memphis, Tennessee. They closed the wound for him, but while he was there, he was told he had malaria.

The wound reopened a short time later, and it would not stay closed. It never would stay closed, so they shipped him to the Veteran's Administration Hospital at Hot Springs, South Dakota. He was there almost a year. That open sore never got any better there; it just got worse.

In September of 1943 Kermit came home to Cherry Creek just before we were to leave for school. When he came home, he said, "I don't have very long." He didn't say, "I don't have very long to live," but he said, "I won't be around very long." I worried about what he meant, but I didn't think he would die!

He said, "I want to get reacquainted with you girls. That is why I came back from Hot Springs." He told us many things like, "You girls should obey Mom and Dad. They had a hard time raising us. You should try to do something in return. You should try to make them proud." Kermit was a good man, and in those few short days he gave me many things to think about.

Soon we went back to school at Immaculate Conception, and Kermit went back to the VA hospital at Hot Springs. In December of 1943 he went back to Cherry

Kermit Swan, high school graduation photograph, 1940.

Creek for good. He refused to go to the VA any more. In letters Mom sent us she said he was getting sicker all the time, but he refused seeing any more doctors or being sent to any more hospitals.

In early April of 1944 Father Mattingly, the priest at Cherry Creek, came after Shirley, Orby, and I at the mission. It was at night when he arrived. He said, "Your brother is not expected to live through the night, so your father would like you children to come home. That is why I am here, to take you back."

So we got ready to leave, and we just left, hardly saying goodbye to anyone. We got home that next morning very early. Instead of driving to the house, Father Mattingly said that first we should go to mass.[82] So we did. We had mass early in the morning and received Holy Communion. Then Father brought us back to the house. Kermit was just lying there. He was skin and bones. There was nothing left to him, but he still recognized us. It was a very sad thing for me to see him like that, to see his terrible suffering. After that I helped Mom take care of him.

Mom and I washed Kermit and his bed clothes every day with water we hauled from the artesian spring. We had to wash his soiled ones every day so we'd have clean linen for the next day. We tried to keep the house very clean, even washing the floors every day. This was the first time I put all the knowledge I had gotten from Grandma to use. I started to cook and bake bread and help Mom all the time. I slept every now and then, and I would talk to Kermit. He used to tell me a lot of things.

He told me, "One of the important things to remember in your life is that you are an Indian. There are girls who go away to school—they don't even stay for a month or two—and when they come home, they say they forgot how to speak their language! That is not right!" He said, "Don't do that. No matter where you go or how long you stay away, you should never forget your Indian language or your Indian ways. You will never become a white person. So don't do that. When girls do that, they are putting on the dog! Don't do that!"

He told me many of the same kinds of things Grandma Julia had told me: "You are not a real pretty girl, but you are a nice looking girl. Don't be chasing after boys like the rest of the girls around here. Some day, no matter what you look like, there will be a man that will come along and he will like you. So don't make a fool of yourself." These were the kinds of things he would tell me when he was strong enough to talk, and we were alone.

One day when he was finished with his words of advice, I asked him, "You always tell us to do things, and we listen to you. We do the things you ask of us. Why don't you go to the hospital and get well, too?" He didn't say anything for a long time. He never did answer.

One morning, the seventh day of May, I think, Kermit was talking to Mom. Soon Mom came to the shade and told Dad that Kermit wanted to go to the hospital. Dad said, "Okay, I'll call the agency hospital and see if they could send an ambulance after him. We'll rest at the agency hospital one night; from there we'll go on to Pierre and let him rest there for a night. From Pierre we'll drive on to Hot Springs." So that was the plan. I was glad Kermit had listened to me. Mom was exhausted, and I wanted so badly for my brother to live.

Soon a hospital car came after Kermit. Mom couldn't go along because she had all us kids and there was no one she cared to leave with us. Dad went along, and pretty soon we heard Kermit was resting well at Cheyenne River Agency Hospital. The next day they took him on to Pierre. Dad called Mr. Griffith, the storekeeper, because he had the only phone in the community. Mr. Griffith came to the house and relayed the message that Kermit was all right and that he would rest the night in Pierre. So the next day we waited for a call from Dad.

Early on the morning of the ninth of May the police came to the house. They gave us the terrible news that Kermit had passed away in the night. He said, "Your brother died about four o'clock this morning in the hospital at Pierre. Your dad said he would be back with the body as soon as he gets the funeral arrangements made."

So my good brother Kermit had died. On the eleventh of May they brought him home to stay. He was in his coffin, dressed in military uniform. Kermit was waked on the eleventh and twelfth of May. On the thirteenth of May 1944 he was buried. Our kind brother, so full of good words for us, was gone. We all took it very hard.

Dad was drunk all the way through the funeral. I think it was the only way he could get through it. When it was over, Mom said, "I'm going to leave that man. Where was James when Kermit and Manuel built this house?" "He's always gone on a trip!" she said, answering her own question. Dad was a tribal councilman at that time, but he'd always been gone a lot, taking census, buying equipment for the tribe, or on the police force. He always took care of us with money; still he was seldom home.

Things like that must have weighed heavy on Mom's heart. She never complained in front of the kids; but when he was drunk at his soldier son's funeral, it was more than Mom could bear. She stayed with Dad, yet it seemed she was never happy with him after that.

It was about a week after the funeral, and Mom had still not eaten anything. "Mom, you'd better eat!" Orby said, but she would not eat. We would fix her different things; still she would not eat. My Aunt Matilda came to talk to her one day. Mom was just sitting there staring off. Aunt Matilda spoke with her for a long time, telling her she must go on, that she still had young children, things like that. Then she fixed Mom something to eat.

Finally, Mom said, "I will eat and try to live, but I wanted to die with Kermit, I loved him so much." She started to eat again, and very gradually she came out of it.

Things weren't good at home for us the rest of that summer. There was a lot of tension between Mom and Dad, and I think I sort of got run down. I guess my parents were having a lot of problems, but I didn't know very much because they kept it fairly well to themselves.

One day Mom said she was going to leave, that she didn't want to be with Dad any more. Different people came by the house and talked with her against the idea of her leaving. My Aunt Mary came from White River to help out. She stayed for a whole month, all of July. Finally, Mom's outlook began to improve. She started to work at the little store and post office in Cherry Creek full time, and that helped.

Dad came back from one of his trips early in August

and told us, "I'm going to take you out to the country place. We haven't been out there all summer, so we'll move out there and wait for Manuel to come home from the war." Manuel had been stationed at the Panama Canal, and he came home on leave in mid-August. His coming home seemed to help, and things between Mom and Dad were better for a while after that.

Manuel was home for about two weeks, and then he left to go back for his final discharge from the army. After he left, my father told us, "You will have to go back to school early because I am going to Texas for the tribe. I'll be gone clear into September. If I don't take you early, there will be no one to take you when it's time."

Shirley, Orby, and I left once again for Immaculate Conception on the eighteenth of August 1944. I was at the mission from August until December, when I got sick. We had to work every day. We worked out in the gardens watering, weeding, and picking produce. Then we canned it all for winter.

It wasn't too bad, spending the remainder of the summer at Stephan, because there were twelve of us who came back early. The Sisters took us to town Saturdays to see a show or shop. Soon the rest of the kids started coming back. This was the time my problems started. I just couldn't gain back the weight I had lost during that hard summer.[83]

🌺   *The Fall of 1944 at Immaculate Conception*

WHEN I WENT back to school in 1944, I was very thin. I tried to comfort myself by thinking, "this was the summer Kermit had died; it had been very strenuous for me; that was why I was so thin." I tried to believe this. When I got to school, the sisters noticed how skinny I was, so they put me to work in the bakery for the next few months. Still, I just could not gain weight, and I kept catching cold.

My "pleurisy" pains were getting worse, too.[84] Every time I would catch cold, the pain from my coughing would be so painful, it was all I could take. Finally, there was a day I was so weak I couldn't get out of bed.

I was lying there in bed crying when Sister Cornelius came in and asked, "What's wrong? Why are you so down?"

So I told her, "I think I'm going to die like Rita, Rosie, and those others."

"Why do you think that?" Sister asked in a comforting voice.

"I have pains in my chest like they did, and now I'm too sick to get up. I don't want to die like they did, far away from my mother and father, not seeing them again." I was crying hard now.

"There, there," Sister said, rubbing my arm. So I had told her, told her of my fear that I had kept inside for almost two years, and I cried and cried.

When I had stopped crying, Sister held my hand and said, "You have been missing a lot of school. Maybe we'll take you down to Fort Thompson and let the doctor have a look at you." So they took me to Fort Thompson that afternoon. It was in the late part of November, and the cold air made it hurt to breathe. A doctor saw me and gave me some tests. He asked me to spit in a cup and took some x-rays of my chest.

I stayed there a few days, and one morning the doctor came in and said, "All of your tests are positive and your lungs are all clouded over.[85] That could be damage from the prairie fire, but you do have tuberculosis."[86] There was that word, that awful dreaded word. My heart sank. I was going to die.

The doctor continued, "Anyway, we are going to send you to a place where you will get well. You can either stay here or go back to the mission at Stephan until your folks come and get you."

"I'd rather stay at the mission," I could barely get the words out. I couldn't see through the tears, I was so scared.

The next day they discharged me and notified my folks. My dad wrote to them and told them he would come after me on the eighteenth or nineteenth of December. He would come with Uncle Dick in his car.

When Dad and Uncle Dick came, neither of them said much. Finally, Dad said, "We have to take you to the Sioux San [sanitorium] right away." I started to cry.[87]

"Why can't I go home for Christmas—and then I can go after that."

"No!" he said. I cried, I wanted to see Mom so bad. "Well, we'll see, after we visit with the doctor at the Agency," he said, trying to comfort me.

Late on the nineteenth of December, we arrived at the Cheyenne River Agency Hospital. Dr. Fleishman examined me, then looked at the charts and x-rays we had brought. Dad asked Dr. Fleishman if I could spend Christmas home with the family. "No!" Dr. Fleishman said firmly, "Your daughter is very sick with TB. We have an epidemic on our hands, and taking her home would endanger her and the whole family. I won't allow it. If you take her home, we'll have to quarantine your house."[88]

Dad said, "Well, that's all right! You just go ahead and quarantine my house. I'll take her home and bring her back before the twenty-eighth, so you can take her to the sanitorium."

Dr. Fleishman was really mad, but he said, "All right! I'll tell you what—I'll let you take her home for Christmas. But on the twenty-eighth of December at eight o'clock, you have her at Dr. Kremer's office in Dupree, and someone will pick her up and take her to the sanitorium."

So Dad said, "Okay." We left for home and a final Christmas with my folks.

When I saw Mom, I started to cry. She looked very sad; holding me, she said, "Some things in life are difficult for us to bear and difficult for us to understand, but we have to go through these even if we don't like it. You're going to get well."

I told her, "I don't ever want to come home again, because I am a disgrace."

She pulled me close to her in her arms; then looking me in the face, fighting back tears, she said, "No! You are not a disgrace to us. Even if you were all covered with sores, I'd still love you. You still would not be a disgrace to us!"

That was all that was said. We had a real nice Christmas. I tried to think positive about living and getting well, but I was scared, scared to be away from my family, scared to be sent to a strange place where people were said to be dying.

Wayeca Win: Lightning Bug Woman

THE DAY BEFORE I was to leave for the sanitorium, Grandma Bridwell came down from her place, on the Dupree mail truck.[89] Dad was looking out the window and said, "Grandma Bridwell is coming from the store." Dad went out into the yard to greet his aunt.

"Nephew," she said, "Why do you have these signs on your house?"

"Madonna is sick with TB. She has to go to the Sioux San. They wanted her to leave before Christmas; but I refused, so they put these red tags on our house. That's why," he told her.

I was sitting inside, but I could hear them. "We'll see about that!" Grandma said. She walked over and tore that red tag off the house. "They don't need to be here," she said angrily. "She's not bad—she's going to get well!" Then she tore off the other one.

To have TB was a big disgrace in those days. They treated those that got TB and their families like they were lepers. Those that didn't have it told their children to stay away from the kids who had TB in their home. The tribal police would put a red tag on any house that had a TB victim living in it. If they died or went to the sanitorium the tags would come off.

I had never heard much about chanhu sica [bad lungs], as it was called in Indian. Some people said it was the same as syphilis, that it was some kind of social disease. Mom and Grandma Bridwell were talking about it. Mom said, "They say wo wa yun zaŋ [social disease] when they talk about people with TB. It cannot be true; it is a lie!"

"Yes, it is a lie," Grandma said. "My mother, Blue Earring Woman, was a strong Indian doctor, and she told me they have nothing to do with each other, except they are white man's diseases."

That's how everybody thought, though. I was a disgrace, and even now I still feel that way at times. I guess it's left over from back then. I first heard of canhu sica in 1940. I had a cousin named Ann Medicine Boy. When she got sick and later died, they said she had quick consumption. A year or two later her brother died from the same thing. They said he had a hemorrhage and bled to death from the mouth. Later they said he had tuberculosis. I had these thoughts, as the minutes with my family passed, waiting to go to the sanitorium.

Part Two

Wani´yetu Ṫōna Oi´yokisilya
(The Years of Sad Isolation or
The Years of Loneliness)

ON DECEMBER 28, 1944, I left for Sioux Sanitorium in Rapid City. Dad had promised Dr. Fleishman that he would have me at Dr. Kremer's office by eight o'clock, and we kept our promise. I started out with Dad and Uncle Dick Swan at six o'clock to meet the hospital car in Dupree. Since we had left so early, we were not in a hurry; and Dad said, "We have some time—let's go over to Grandma Bridwell's place."

Grandma Bridwell was already up, building a fire in her wood cook stove, when we got there. She heard the car pull up into her yard and came out to greet us. She said, "You come into the house, and I'll make you breakfast and coffee. You must be on your way to Dupree."

I started to cry, and Dad told her, "Madonna is frightened. Today is the day she has to go to the sanitorium. We have to take her to Dupree to meet the hospital car, and then they take her to the Sioux San."

"Oh, my little Donna," she said turning towards me; her eyes were suddenly sad. She put her arms out, and I ran to her. She hugged me and told me not to cry.

She took me into the little room where she had her bed. "Tell me what has you so frightened, Donna?" she asked softly. We sat down on her bed, and she took my hand.

"Because I have TB, and I'm going away from Mom for a long time, maybe forever. I'll probably die over there. I'm such a disgrace to my family. I feel so dirty and ashamed," I told her between sobs.

"Now, Donna, you're not going to die, and as far as being a disgrace, if you're a disgrace, then there must be a lot of them around here. Nearly every family in Cherry Creek, Red Scaffold, perhaps all of Cheyenne River Reservation has had to send relatives to the sanitorium. Your mom and dad love you. We all love you! You are no disgrace. You will get well and come home!" she said, looking into my eyes.

Sioux Sanitorium, Rapid City, South Dakota, ca. 1944.

"I feel like such a bother, and now I feel like a baby crying in front of you," I told her.

Then she preached to me, saying, "Donna! You go there and be brave. When you come back, you can stay with your mom and dad and never leave. You do what the doctors tell you and pray every day. You'll come home! I'll come and visit you in the san," she said quietly, as she rubbed my back and tried to blot my tears with a cloth.[1]

We went back into the main room, and Grandma finished making breakfast. I wasn't very hungry, but Dad and Uncle Dick ate everything. When they had finished, Dad said, "Thanks for the breakfast and for helping Madonna."

"Oh, can I ride down there with you?"[2] she asked, stepping towards Dad. She waited for his answer.

"Sure, if you want to. You're certainly welcome to," was his reply.

When we got to Dr. Kremer's office, the hospital car wasn't there yet. Grandma said, "While we wait, I'm going to pray." She took out a small pipe. She sang softly, put tobacco in it, then lit it. She took a puff and handed it to Dad and Uncle Dick and then me. Then she prayed, "Grandfathers, please let the medicines of the white doctors help Madonna. Grandfathers, help her to get well; Grandfathers, help her to be brave. Grandfathers, let the older people in the hospital watch over her and teach her well."

Then the hospital car came from the agency. Mr. Lewis was driving the car. He noticed the little pipe Grandma was putting back in her bag. He smiled in approval. Mr. Lewis was also an Indian, from Oklahoma, so he didn't say anything. So we left Dad, Uncle Dick, and Wayeca Win standing in the road waving. I waved back, trying to smile, as I fought back tears that blurred my sight.

When we got to the door of the san, the place that was to be a prison for me for more years than I could have imagined, Mr. Lewis broke the awful silence. He said, "You are going to be admitted now. It's a nice place. In fact, they have earphones for every bed, so you can listen to radio shows.[3] You can finish this year by correspondence, and then you will have only your junior and senior years to finish when you get out. So you stay here and get well. I've looked at your grades, and when you get out you can go on to be a nurse like you want.[4] Don't give up your dreams. You'll live—you will get well!" Mr. Lewis really preached to me. "Good luck," he finally said. He shook my hand and turned to leave.

Grandma Bridwell was a traditional full-blood woman, married to a white man. She was a very good person and well liked by everyone. Grandma Bridwell, Wayeca Win, Lightning Bug Woman, was killed in a car wreck; she never got to visit me, but I'll never forget her!

I stood there, alone now—alone and frightened because of my TB. Finally I opened the door, took the papers Mr. Lewis had given me, my little suitcase, and walked in.

 Sioux Sanitorium

AFTER MR. LEWIS left me at the door, I stood there wishing I could just run away, but I stayed and was admitted. I was really lonely that first night. I cried and cried. They put me in a private room, and I was lying there sobbing. Somebody came up behind me and called my name. I jumped! I didn't think anybody knew me up there. I turned over

Madonna Swan at Sioux Sanitorium, 1946.

and saw it was Margaret Halfred. She was very skinny, her
skin was yellow, and she was in a wheelchair.

Margaret had been my cousin's girlfriend and had been
a pretty girl. As I looked at her, I couldn't stop thinking
about how awful she looked. Thirty years old, and to look

like this! Just seeing her there made me feel more scared than I had ever been in my life. "I heard you were here, Madonna, so I had to come visit you," she said.

The nurse left us alone, and I sobbed as I told her how lonely and frightened I felt in this place. Margaret tried to comfort me, telling me that this was not such a bad place, that the staff were good people. It didn't help—just seeing what she had become made me fearful. "You won't be alone!" she said. "There are many people who are here that you know. You can visit them, and they will visit you. You should ask the doctor if you can get into one of the wards, so you won't be alone," she told me, still trying to comfort me. "There is an empty bed in our ward; maybe you can come there. I would like that," she said weakly.

During the next few days Margaret came fairly often, bringing me bananas, oranges, candy, and books. After a while I didn't cry anymore. Soon I was moved into her ward. She was the first person to die while I was there. She was really sick. Finally, one day she couldn't get up any-more, so the nurses had to help her sit up. They had to feed her, but soon they just moved her out.

I asked where they had moved her to. "We moved her to a private room," the nurse told me. I asked if I could see her. "Yes, but only for a few minutes at a time; she is very sick!" was her reply. I went over to her room and found her near death. Margaret Halfred died eight days after I was admitted. When I saw her that first night, I realized this was a place for people to die. There were several other patients on the floor, just like Margaret, who were very thin and so pale. I felt very bad; the feelings of loneliness and fear didn't go away.

❧ *Mary Brown*

So IT WENT on this way, day in, day out. One day I walked into a room where there were some younger girls. I met a girl in this room named Mary Brown, who was a Blackfoot from Montana. She must have sensed my feelings, because she tried to talk to me, saying, "Don't feel so lonely anymore, so much like you're going to die; you can get well. You have to rest and take your cod-liver oil, and you'll get well!"

I think Mary was really good for me; she brought me out of my dumps. She had a good sense of humor, and we became great friends. Soon we were joined by a girl named Bernice Long, who was from Bridger, a girl I had known for some time. Then the three of us chummed around together. We knew we were all in this boat together. Gradually my feelings of despair and fear became less a part of my thinking. Mary was at the san for three or four years. I can't recall exactly what became of her. She had TB of the skin and would break out a lot. There wasn't much wrong with her lungs, yet all of a sudden one day they took her away.

We were not separated into wards by the seriousness of our condition. We were all in together, the sick ones with

Madonna with friends from Sioux Sanitorium, 1947. From left to right: Irene Hill, Mary Brown, Cora, Carrie Two Heart, and Madonna.

the not-so sick-ones. I guess those of us who were highly positive kept reinfecting those that had negative sputum cultures. They should have divided or separated us so we didn't reinfect the healthier ones, but they didn't. I felt bad about that.

I finished the correspondence courses that spring, finishing the eighth grade. That was all the education I got. We high school-aged girls asked the administration about school; yet they would just tell us that there was no money for school, and there was nobody that would come to teach us here anyway. The san had a therapist that taught us to embroider, crochet, knit, or paint. That was all we did. Time passed so slowly that loneliness for my family stayed with me, growing all the time, like a hunger that would not leave.

The nurses and staff were kind, for the most part, but they were afraid of us, afraid of our disease; they seldom touched us and always wore masks. They never really did boss us around; we were there more or less on our own. The staff would make bed checks and find us for our medication, which we rarely got. All we took was that awful cod-liver oil every morning, and that was it.

                                        Bean Bags

OUR TREATMENT also involved the placing of bean bags on our chest. Each of us had a certain number we were supposed to use. The bean bags were on our chest for hours each day. They were supposed to partially collapse our lungs to restrict the air reaching our lungs and kill the germ. We would lie with four or five of these bags on our chests for hours each day, but it never did any good.

The days went by, one by one; the routine seldom varied. I got up in the morning, went to the bathroom, washed up, and brushed my teeth. We only bathed on certain days—a bath or shower, depending on how sick we were. If I had a depressing or bad day, I would bathe and wash my hair; it made me feel a little better, a little more human.

Breakfast was always at 7:30. We wore pajamas and house coats all the time; [we] dressed all alike, like the inmates at the penitentiary in Sioux Falls, all dressed in stripes. I guess that was intended to keep us from escaping. If we could escape, we could not get far. Of course, our regular clothes were locked away.

In the later years, after years of pleading, the staff allowed us to purchase material and make our own pajamas and house coats. It was 1946 before they changed that rule; then we could wear our own clothes, pajamas, and house coats. At least we didn't all have to dress alike any more.

There were no patients going out on leave or dismissed in 1944 or 1945. Not until 1946 did the first few patients leave alive. Death was the only way anybody left before that, and there were many. I had a diary, and in it I wrote down the little things that happened each day, things girls outside the san would never have bothered to write down. I wrote down whatever happened, no matter how ordinary, things like the kind of day it was, how I felt, and if an outsider came to visit. I wrote down why and when they came, and I wrote down the names of those that had died.

Bernice Long also kept a diary. These were a daily log for us. In 1950 we went through our diaries together. We counted five hundred deaths. That was only a count of the deaths we heard of and did not include those who died at the san that we didn't hear of, or those that went home and later died, or those who ran away and died.

It seemed that when one would die, two more would die soon after.[5] That was something both of us had noted in our diaries. When one would die, we would wonder who the other two would be. We wrote that at varied times, always wondering if the next one would be us or one of our friends.

Corn Meal, Corn Ball

EVERY DAY WE ATE breakfast, the usual bowl of cornmeal mush. After breakfast we got our usual cupful of cod-liver oil mixed with tomato juice. It makes me sick to think about it even now, yet it was the only "medicine" we ever got!

After breakfast I had to bathe two of the women who were too sick to bathe themselves. We did this every day. Some days there would be more to bathe than others. On this day I had two to wash; when I had finished, I had to wash the hair of two women on "death row," so I didn't have to make any beds that day. I didn't care much for making beds, especially if the person couldn't get out, because it was so strenuous. We always helped out with the sick ones, I guess, because they were short of staff.

I finished washing their hair and went back to our ward for lunch. At one o'clock every day the nurses came, and we got our "therapy." Therapy was when they made us lie down, and they would put bean bags on our chests. I was prescribed four pounds of bean bags for my therapy. I guess the bags were supposed to partially collapse our lungs and kill the germ by cutting down on the amount of oxygen the germ got. It never did that, kill the germ, even though we did this every day for years.

We would have to lie still for three to four hours with the bean bags on our chests. By the time supper came and those bean bags were put away, we'd be feeling pretty frisky. This night we got macaroni and corn bread. That same old doughy corn bread. It was about an inch thick and just doughy!

I rolled my corn bread into a little hard ball and said, "Oh, no! Doughy corn bread again!" I just bounced that corn ball on my tray. The girls laughed real loud.

A minute later a mean old nurse named Mrs. Peterson came in. "So! What is so funny here?" she asked.

"This!" I said, and just threw that corn ball at her. I knocked her cap off!

Madonna Swan and Rachel Red Owl, 1948.

"Why! Why! Why!" she stuttered and spit. She bent over and looked for that corn ball and picked it up.

She looked at that corn ball and asked, "What is this?"

Just as she said that, Mary Brown yelled, "How would you like to eat this?" and threw her corn bread at Mrs. Peterson. It smacked her real hard right in the chest and fell with a thud to the floor. Nurse Peterson got real mad and red in the face, and she stomped out of the room.

We howled so hard we could have had a hemorrhage! Anyway, we got restricted to our ward for two weeks. We had to stay in and not go anywhere or do anything for two weeks. That corn ball gave us all a little vacation!

                                    Death Row

THERE WAS a place on the east side of the san we called "death row." There were private rooms. Whenever you were placed in there, you knew you were a goner.[6] I remember one time they took this old woman in from Bridger and put her on "death row." I heard there was a new patient in from the reservation. I asked a nurse who this new patient was.

"She is an old woman from the Bridger community, and she is very sick. She is not expected to live very long. Her name is Mrs. Curley." She was an aunty of mine. I knew she was very old and didn't speak a word of English.

That night Bernice Long and I decided to go see our aunty. Mrs. Curley remembered me. I could see it in her eyes. She looked very frightened. I asked her in Indian, "Do you remember me, aunty?"

"Yes, you are Lucy's daughter. I heard you were up here," she said weakly in Indian. Bernice introduced herself, and we sat there and spoke with her for a while.

Soon she looked up at me and said, "Granddaughter, I want you to do something for an old woman who is going to die from this chanhu sica, and I want to go home to die. Please call my son at Bridger and tell him I want to go home to die."

I told her, "Well, I don't know what we can do or how we could call him, but we will try."

We left her lying there, so frightened and alone. We talked over her problem and decided to talk to Gloria Traversy about it. Gloria was an Indian nurse from home, and she was always kind to us. We told her we wanted to call Mrs. Curley's son, and why.

"Yea, that's fine. You could call up the Howe's store and see if the storekeeper can find him," she said. "I will look the other way when you use the phone!"

We called the store and told the storekeeper to get hold of the Curleys. "Tell them Mrs. Curley is very near death and that she wants to die at home. At least they could be with her when she dies."

The man said, "Sure thing! I'll get down there this afternoon and tell them. I'll call you back tomorrow and let you know if they are on their way."[7]

"Thanks for your help," I said and hung up.

The next morning the storekeeper called back and

said, "Mrs. Curley's people are on their way. They should be there by this afternoon or evening." But they never showed up. Bernice and I went back to see Mrs. Curley. I could tell she was going downhill quickly. By late afternoon she was really down. She kept saying, "I wish they would hurry up." We just kept telling her, "They will be here soon. They are on their way. They're coming soon now." But they never did.

After a while Father Zimmerman came in, and he asked us to stay. So we did. He administered the last rites and anointed her forehead with oil. She called to me, so I put my ear close to her mouth. Her voice was just above a whisper, she was so weak.

"Please, please say the Our Father in Indian for me." I never said the Our Father in Indian because we were never allowed to say it that way at school.

"I can't. I don't know it in Indian," I said to the Father.

He smiled and said, "Oh, it's easy. Look on page 158," handing me the missal. "It's real easy, I'll help you."

Father helped me, and we gave the old woman her last wish. Just as we got through, she took her last breath. It was a good thing we were there, her only family in her last moments. "Well, at least she heard her prayer in Indian before she went," I thought to myself. At least we could do that for her.

Her family showed up the next day. They had been held up in Sturgis until it was too late, too late to spend the last minutes with their mom on "death row."

                    Avril Backward

SOMETIMES I WOULD sink deep into a pit of despair, not do anything, just give up eating until I would die of starvation, I hoped. Those were terrible days, adjusting to the idea of being away from family, confined indoors, waiting to die.

Particularly awful were the times right after we got the

results of our three-month sputum and x-ray tests. If we didn't get any good news, and I never did, that's when we felt very low. It was like seeing the parole board and always being told maybe next time.

We had a roommate named Avril Backward. She was from Pine Ridge and really a good person. She was teaching us how to do lazy-stitched beadwork. We wanted to make miniature moccasins, just for practice. Avril had kind of an elderly mom, what today you might call a real traditional woman. Avril's mom got us some sinew for thread, some beads, and buckskin. She made us some awls by pushing a heavy common needle into a cherry wood stick. I remember she said, "Ho! Now I brought you girls some beads and things. So now you can go to work." She fixed that sinew for us, softening it, separating the little threads, and then wetting and rolling them straight and thin. She had brought a bunch of sinew and made enough for all of us.

That is what Avril was doing one day, teaching us how to get the design right and the rows of beads straight. We used to get up early and all get ready to bead. We'd all sit on Avril's bed and start our beadwork. There was Dora Breast, Mary Brown, Bernice, and I, and, of course, Avril; we could all go up to her bed and talk and laugh and do our beadwork.

Avril was said to be getting better and was supposed to go home soon. On this particular day we were doing just that, getting our sinew, beads, and awls out to start beading. We all sat on Avril's bed. Somebody said something funny, and Avril really laughed. She just threw her head back and laughed loudly. Suddenly she brought her head forward and blood started to come from her mouth.

I screamed, "Avril!"

Then Bernice yelled, "Avril, here is some Kleenex!" Avril wiped her face and just stared at the blood on it.

I think she panicked because she looked at it and just kept saying, "What? What?" in disbelief. Then her head went around in a circle, and she fell back on the bed. Dora rang and rang the bell for the nurse.

Soon the nurse came running down the hall. Mrs. Kurt, the head nurse, came in first, took one look at Avril, and ran out. Soon she returned with the doctor. They rushed in and unplugged Avril's earphones, cleared off her bed, and told Avril to lie still. They cranked her bed up and wheeled her out.

Dora said, "I'm going to follow. You girls stay here." About half an hour later, Dora came back in crying uncontrollably.

"She's dead! She's dead!" was all she could say. "They told us she was well, and now she is dead!" she screamed. "She must not have been well; otherwise, she would not have had that," was all I could think. "Maybe we'll all end up like that, choking to death on our own blood."

Later, when we were calmer, we sat there talking about how it seemed that when they told one of us we were well, that we could still die. I said, "Maybe we'll be getting ready to go home and just from the excitement, we'll have an attack and die just like Avril." This was a very low time for me, for all of us.

Living in the san would make you feel like an outcast with some filthy disease like leprosy. We couldn't go outside. We were allowed only to stand out on the little balconies and look out across to Rapid City, watching people go about their daily lives, enjoying life. From 1944, through 1945 and 1946, until 1947, we were not allowed to go outdoors, not stand on the ground, Maka Ina, Mother Earth, even once. Just going to the window or a balcony was all we could do, but even that was a relief—at least it was fresh air.

                         An Investigation at the San

WE ATE BEANS for almost every meal at the san. They were getting rations in those days, so that is what we got. We ate a lot of corn meal mush and corn bread, too. Once in a while we'd get yellow corn meal with brown specks in it. They sure looked like mouse droppings, so we'd complain; but they never did anything about it. They would not listen to us.

One evening we were being served our meal. In the ward next to ours we had some friends. There was Eva Two Bulls, Eleanor Lafferty, Ione Wada, and Lucille Night. They always got their supper a few minutes before we did. Like every night, we could hear the trays clattering on the cart. A moment later one of the girls screamed. Eleanor ran into the room and said, "Girls! Girls! Don't eat your soup. There's something in it!" We looked at each other and pushed our beans aside.

Wanda Arpan burst into the room next. She was holding up something on a napkin and told us to look at it. "It's a mouse!" she said. "It was in the beans!" I took one look, turned away, and got sick.

While I was getting finished being sick, Wanda and Eleanor ran downstairs to the kitchen. I guess that cook was really mad at them. She screamed and cursed at them and tried to get that mouse, but the girls kept it and ran back upstairs.

A nurse came in a moment later and said, "What are all you girls doing in here? What's all this about a mouse? You have the whole floor in an uproar! Let me see it then. Now!" Wanda held up the napkin.

"See!" she said defiantly. The nurse grabbed for it, but Wanda was too quick. "Oh, no you don't! I'm going to show this to the authorities!" Wanda said angrily. "We'll call Pierre or write or something!" she kept yelling at the nurse. "We told you we saw turds in the food, and now a mouse. I suppose a mouse is good for us!" We all laughed, and the nurse went out shaking her head.

The next day the girls got to a phone somehow and called Pierre. Wanda came in the room that afternoon grinning from ear to ear. "We called the Sanitation and Health Department!" she said. "They are going to send somebody here by Wednesday. I hope that mouse lasts till then," she giggled. We all laughed at her joke. "Well, at least maybe the food would improve, and any improvement would be just fine," I thought. We didn't eat much that week.

Wednesday morning about eleven, a tall woman and two men in suits came to talk to Wanda, so we all went into her ward. Dr. Sedlechek and the head nurse and ward clerk came, too.[8]

"So, what is all this business about a mouse?" Sedlechek asked angrily. Wanda reached under her bed and took out the napkin with that dried up baby mouse in it.

"Here! Here is the mouse," Wanda said. Sedlechek tried to look first, but the lady from the Health Department took it.

"It sure looks like a baby mouse to me," she said.

"I can assure you we had nothing to do with this!" Sedlechek said, in his most convincing voice.

"Well, I'll take it and have it analyzed, but it sure looks like a baby mouse with dried up beans on it to me," she said, glaring at Sedlechek.

Next, the tall woman said, "I'd like to take a look at your kitchen." So they left. They went downstairs to the kitchen and looked through the food bins. Those bins were infested with mice.

The lady soon came back upstairs, and as she threw the mouse in the trash, she said, "Well, I guess we won't have to keep that anymore. That kitchen was filthy and full of mice nests. You'll be getting your meals from the outside for a while. They are going to have to close, clean, and rebuild that kitchen before they can cook here again. And they'll have to get inspected by us before they reopen!" she said, smiling at me. I smiled back at her, and she turned and walked out.

So Wanda and Eleanor had caused quite a ruckus, and they didn't even get put on restrictions. I learned that when you are right, it pays to stand up and defend yourself. The food was a little better after that. At least it didn't have hair and mouse turds in it!

※   *Levi In The Woods*

I FIRST MET LEVI In The Woods in 1942. We were both real young then, so we used to write notes to each other. I would answer his notes with a note. We never spoke face to face. That is what we did all summer—wrote notes back and forth and used friends to exchange the notes. I never thought much about it, but it was fun. One time towards fall, my father found one of these notes.

"How long have you been getting them?" he asked.

"I've been getting them all summer," I told him.

He said, "You know, when a man is sincere about a woman, he will come to the girl's home to visit them. If they are not sincere, this is the way they do it, like Levi. You better be careful," he said.

So I told him, "We never saw each other or anything, you know."

"Well, that's all right, but in the future you better bring them to the house," he said.

I went back to school that fall. When I came back that spring, it was Memorial Day, and they were having a big dance that night. The hall was about four hundred yards from our house, so we went over there. When we went anywhere with the folks, we had to go inside and stay there and watch whatever was going on, whether we were bored, whether we liked it or not.

We were sitting, watching the dancers move around the floor. Later that evening Levi's mom came over to talk to me and said, "Sonny would like to see you, just for a few minutes. I'm going to give you this plate of food for him."

I told her, "Oh, Mom won't let me go!"

Levi's mom answered, "Oh, I'll try to speak with her anyway." She went over and spoke with Mom, and my mother didn't say anything for a while.

Finally, she said, "Oh, I guess she can, for a few minutes." So I took the plate of food and went out.

Levi's mom had told me he was parked on the southeast

side of the hall, so that's where I went. He was about the same age as me. Levi was sitting in his dad's car. Until then I had never talked to him in person. I was kind of bashful and backward. As I walked over to where he was sitting, he rolled down his window.

I laughed and said, "Your mom told me to bring you this food."

He laughed back and said, "I'm not that hungry!" We both chuckled. Then he said, "Well, give it to me anyway."

Levi took the plate in the car; then he got out and went around to the other side and opened the door. He said, "Why don't you sit in here with me for a while, and we'll visit."

I told him, "No, I better not; my mom and dad will get mad. I'll just visit you from here."

"No. Just come and sit for a little while," he pleaded. I got in and sat down. He started asking me how I was, how I liked being back from school, things like that.

I told him about school. He spoke Indian to me, so I spoke to him in Indian. He said, "Gee, it's funny—you stay away for nine months at a time, and when you come home, you haven't forgotten how to speak Indian. Some of the girls around here go away for a month, and they come back and can't talk Indian." So we were laughing and talking about things like that, and sure enough, here came my mom.

She was looking around, and finally she came over and said to me, "I think you better come back inside now. Your dad will get mad at you."

So I told Levi, "Well, I better go."

Levi said, "Some time I'll come by and see you."

So I said, "Why don't you do that. The folks won't mind, if you come over to the house to visit."

Later that summer Levi started coming to our house. I used to visit with him. Several times that summer he came to visit me. Eventually, I got so I really liked him. One time, towards the fall, he said, "As long as you are going to school, I'm going to go to school also. When we graduate, we'll get married."

I was very happy, and I said, "OK!"

He went on, "By that time you'll have your Sioux bene-fit money, and I'll get mine.[9] That will give us enough to get married."

I agreed, "All right! We'll do that!"

In those days things were different; all we had ever done was talk to each other. My folks always told me that the girls don't wrestle with the boys. They said, "You don't do those things. You have to be respectful in all ways."

Once in a while Levi would get to teasing me and poke me in the side with his finger. But I told him, I'd say, "Oh, don't do that. That's not nice." So he didn't do that anymore.

That fall was when I started to get sicker and sicker at school. Finally I had to go to the Sioux San in Rapid City. Before I went, I spent my last Christmas with my family. I didn't see Levi, because I was ashamed, but I wrote and told him, "Don't come and see me; I am very contagious.[10] I could spread my germ to you or anybody that comes near me. I won't be able to see you." I told him, "I guess that this is the end of our childhood dreams of getting to-gether, of getting married. I'm a disgrace to all humanity now that I've caught tuberculosis. It is really a bad disease, and you shouldn't bother writing to me anymore."

Levi wrote a letter back to me and said, "It isn't that way! You are not a disgrace, and I still care for you. If you go to the sanitorium, I will wait for you." I wrote back to him and told him not to visit me or write to me. After I went to the san, Levi would write to me now and then, but I would never answer his letters. I figured he could find someone better than me, and besides, I thought, "who knows when, or if, I'll ever get out of this place."

    Levi's Mom Comes to Visit: 1947

IN 1947 I got word from Dr. Sedlechek that I would not be allowed to go home for Christmas. I was feeling pretty good then, and I really wanted to get away from the san for a while.

One afternoon, Levi's mother came to visit me. We visited, and soon she said, "I'm here to check you out. You and Levi are going to get married and then you can come back."

I was surprised, and I told her, "You'll have to ask my Dad."

But she said, "No, if we can do it without letting him know, then we will. You are of age."

I said, "Yes, if it is what Levi wants. I still care for him very much."

Mrs. In The Woods tried to check me out, but they wouldn't let her. They told her, "Under no circumstances will we let her leave. She is a sick girl!"

So I didn't leave, and I didn't get married. Before she left to go back to Cherry Creek she brought Levi to see me. It was very hard, but I told him, "You should look for another girlfriend, because it's going to be a long time before I get out of here. You know you shouldn't have to wait that long. So you should go ahead and find a good woman and get married."

Levi quietly turned and left the room. Maisy, his mom, said, "Oh, I don't think he will find another woman; he cares only for you. If you write to him, he won't even look; he'll wait." I never did write to him or answer his letters. Soon after that he met Doris Ward and married her later that spring.

In the spring of 1947, I was doing well, and they said I could get a pass to leave the san for a week. So I came home for a week at Easter. That's the time I met Jay Abdalla for the first time. Shirley and I went to a big dance up at Dupree and that is where I met him.

Jay said, "I've been looking all over for you. I was your brother Kermit's buddy during the war. I promised him if anything happened to him, I would look after you."

I didn't think anything about what Jay said because Shirley told me that this Jay drank a lot. Jay was half Arab and half Yankton Sioux.[11] Shirley told me, "He always has a good job and a nice car." I didn't think much about meeting him. After staying at the dance a short time, we came home.

I think I was going to go back to the san on a Wednesday. I was going to catch the mail truck to Dupree and from there catch a bus back to the san. Mom and Dad were going to ride to Dupree with me. Levi was already married then, but he sent me a letter. My dad got the letter, and when he gave it to me he said, "This man is already married, so you shouldn't answer the letter. You can read it but don't answer it."

I read the letter and in it he said, "I got married, but I don't love the woman I'm married to. I married her because she is going to have my baby. That is why I married her. After you told me that you would never be able to marry me, I got discouraged and took up with Doris. As long as I live, I'll always have you in my heart." He said, "I hope you do that, too. Maybe someday we'll be able to be together."

In 1948, about a year after that, Levi was killed. They told me he died fixing a car. The jack fell and the car hit him on the chest. When they pulled him out, he was bleeding from the mouth. He choked on his own blood and died.

 The Crow Girls Eat Peyote

I WAS LYING DOWN, looking out of the window, wondering about things like how many people had died here. How many bodies I had seen taken out of the door across the courtyard beneath my window[12]—all Lakota people, mostly good people, who had harmed no one. Why had God done this? Why was I here so long?

Today three bodies had been taken out. I heard one of the men was from Cheyenne River, although I did not hear his name until later. I thought back over all those years I had been there. The roomies who had died, those who had left, chums brought together by pain and sickness—I usually thought of the other people as the sick ones, the ones who might die and be put out near the back door, to be taken to the reservations, buried at home among their families.

When I thought of myself, I always tried to think positive, like I would go home. The Crow girls were positive, especially the ones who ate peyote. Our priest in Cherry Creek had told us about the peyote eaters, and I had heard Dad and Uncle Dick Swan talk about it once. These Crow girls would wait until after the night matron had finished her rounds. Then they would go to the ladies' room and sit in the shower stall and eat their peyote and sing songs and pray.

One night these girls invited me and my chum Bernice Long to come to their meeting. I was kind of scared and I didn't want to get caught. "They'll put us on restrictions!" I tried to tell them.

"So what?" one of the tougher girls answered. "What could they really do to us? Nothing."

Bernice bumped my arm and said to me in Indian, "These Crow girls might get rough with us if we changed our mind, and besides, they seem to get better and leave. Maybe that herb they eat does help them."

We went with them, giggling and joking about getting caught. When we got to the shower room, the Crow girls said to sit down. One girl got a glass of water while another took out a bag of cedar and a bag of little green cactus buttons. Another girl took a small metal frying pan and built a little fire with match sticks. Then she sprinkled cedar on it and smudged the bag with the peyote in it.

The girls began to pass the peyote. I could tell from the faces they were making that this peyote did not taste too good. When it got to Bernice she took one out, sniffed it, and put it in her mouth. I watched closely and she really made a face. Then she spit it out and ran for the door, and

I followed. We could hear the Crow girls giggling as we
ran back towards our ward. I smiled at the memory as I lay
there looking at the spring rains soaking the san grounds.

A Birthday to Forget: 1948

JUNE, JULY, AUGUST, September passed, and still I had
not been given any good news. After seeing Mom in April,
I wanted to go home even worse than ever. I was feeling
good. Not quite as good as in April—I now weighed only
120 pounds, but I felt good.[13] That morning I fixed six
or seven beds and then sponge-bathed a couple of the
sicker ones.

Later that day I got a letter from Mom. She said Dad
was coming and that he was bringing a special birthday
present from the whole family. She said, "I hope you like
your present," and closed with some news about Cherry
Creek and her usual prayer: "I pray every morning and
every night that you will come home to stay. The whole
family and many others are praying for you. Please keep
praying and don't give up hope."

Dad was supposed to come that day, so I sat there in
the ward, waiting. It was a warm day, and the steam heat
overheated the room. It made me feel more short of
breath than usual, so I pushed up the window. A cracking
or popping sound, like bubble gum, came from my chest,
and a pain shot up my arm. It took me by surprise, and
when Lorraine came in a moment later to ask me down to
their ward for a good card game, I was still sitting there.

"In a moment. I just want to sit here and rest for a
minute," I said. It was hard for me to catch my breath,
to talk.

"Oh, chum, I didn't know you had a cold," Lorraine
said. Something warm and salty came up my throat. It
made me cough and I spit it out. Lorraine shouted, "You're
hemorrhaging! Lay down!" she said, as she lay my head

back on the bed. "Nurse! Nurse!" she yelled. "Come quick—Donna is sick!"

A nurse came in to help, but I just kept bleeding and coughing, drowning in my own blood. I gasped for air between coughs, my ribs ached, and my eyes watered. I felt as if a tight band was crushing my chest, tightening down on my lungs.

They packed my chest in ice. Oh, I hated that terrible pain! I didn't care if I died.[14] At least this terrible pain would be over with. Somehow I remembered the letter Mom had sent, and it made me want to pray. I prayed either to die right away or get well. I just could not take this any longer.

Still I kept coughing and bleeding. About six that evening the blood stopped coming up, and they took me from that ice. I was scared and lonely. I hated myself for not getting well. It was all that night, the next day, and finally the next night before they let me go back to my ward. At least there I was with my friends, but the feeling that I would probably die would not leave me.

When Dad was allowed to see me, he looked very sad and said, "Donna, don't worry. They are going to take a new set of x-rays. Try not to think about anything until they are made." He brought a blue footlocker with him and set it on my bed.

"Open it," I said, finally distracted for a minute. I wanted to see what Mom's surprise was. Inside the trunk was a dark Pendleton blanket with deep red fringe, like a shawl. In the bottom of the trunk was a tanned buffalo robe! Aunt Mary from White River had sent it.

Dad said, "The buffalo are sacred to our people. Aunt Mary is a wise woman; she sent the robe so that it might bring you back to health."

I asked Dad to put it over me. It felt so good, so warm, soft, and furry. Dad looked down at me, a tear in his eye. He touched my hand and said, "I hope you like your presents."

"I do," I said. As he turned to leave, I grabbed his hand and said, "Bring Mom next time.[15] Please!?"

"We'll see, we'll see," he said, and left.

 Easter at Home: 1948

I WAS LAST home in 1947; and then around April of 1948, I asked if I could go home for Easter, and they said "Yes"! The folks were living in the country then, and I couldn't wait to see all the changes on the place I had read so much about. I couldn't wait to see Mom. I had seen her only once in four years, and my heart ached for the chance to see her, to feel her in person. In the back of my mind I hoped secretly also that somehow I would not have to come back here ever again.

"Why did I have to be here so long? My whole life would be gone, and I would still be here!" I told the doctor. I weighed 148 pounds. I looked like early pictures of my mom. I thought, "If they're going to let me go home I must be getting better! I tried to console myself.

Dad came to get me in an automobile. It was only the second time I had taken a ride or even been outdoors in years. I cried with tears of quiet joy at each passing hill, past the stores at Union Center and White Owl, past the familiar places I had traveled in my mind so many times in recent days.

The cactus were getting ready to bloom. Everything smelled so good. Oh, how I prayed to God that I was well, that nothing would go wrong. Dreams of life on the outside welled up in me. The thought of ever living away from Mom and my family filled me with fear. "Oh, well, I feel real well," I thought.

I was sure I was cured, that my next test would mean freedom. I had felt well for quite some time and could not understand why they would not let me away from the "sick

Madonna with her family, Easter, 1948. Back row: Orby, Cousin James Swan, and Madonna; front row: James Hart Swan and Lucy Swan.

ones." Maybe, just maybe, I've caught it again because I have to stay in the san.

I fell asleep but woke as we approached a washed-out area near our old turnoff. I could see the house made of logs! Oh, it was real nice! Mom came out as the car approached. We ran to each other, tears streaming. We hugged and hugged.

"Mew, Mew," Mom cried quietly. "Cinksi, mi cinksi! (Daughter, my daughter!)"

"Ina, Ina! (Mother, Mother!)"—my throat pinched off any other words.

Then I hugged Manuel. "So strange not to hug Kermit," I thought. That would have made it perfect. Old Uncle Frank Council Bear and my Uncle Dick Swan and Cousin Mary and the Thunder Hoop family were all there. They didn't act frightened of me—they made me feel so good. We had a happy dinner of wojapi, wigliunkagapi, wastunkala, all kinds of things, foods we never had at the sanitarium. Everyone was so happy, catching me up on everything and everyone.

Mom prayed at dinner, prayed that I would come home to stay. We ate and teased and joked and ate. Somehow, except for everyone looking older, it seemed just the way I had imagined it in my mind as I lay awake nights at the san.

People came and went all day every day, always to see Donna and wish me well. They came to eat and tell me of their children or lives or old gossip. I didn't care what they had to say. I was hungry to catch up, to feel a part of my people, these people. I heard many glad things but more sad things. I heard of deaths from TB, of hard winters and little food, of boys lost in the war.

I was beginning to feel like Donna again. I looked in the mirror. I looked good, I thought—Yes! The best I've looked in years, or maybe ever! I was tall and I weighed 148 pounds. I stood there thinking that the weight gave me a grown up shape I was proud of. Mom had made me some dresses that helped me to feel grown up. So many years had slipped by, it was hard for me to see myself as a young woman. I felt more grown up now than I had ever felt. After all, I was twenty years old, and had never gotten myself "fixed up" for a dance, for a man, for anyone! Mom seemed to understand, as she stood there smiling softly with me looking into the mirror.

Later that day we went out in a wagon to see Manuel's cattle. He was so proud of his little herd. He even said, "I sure miss you, Donna." "A lot for Manuel to say," I couldn't help but think, yet I soaked up every word. I felt like my heart, my soul, soaked up everything!

A cold breeze came up from the southwest that morning. It took my breath away, but I chose not to notice or care. I was alive again, outside those brick prison walls. By the time we got back, I felt like I had to cough. I fought it, fought back with every fiber of my body. "Please, dear God, don't let me be sick now, don't let me cough," I said in a prayer to myself.

By five o'clock I couldn't hold it back any longer. It started, that damned cough! Everyone pretended not to notice. Mom told me to sit near the vaporizer on the wood stove, but she looked very concerned. She spoke so gently. I could see clearly, now, Grandma High Pine's manner in my mother. She had aged; small wrinkles had started to fill the spaces between the lines of her face.

I couldn't stop coughing. Dad borrowed the car from Uncle Dick. Then he and Mom brought me to the doctor in Phillip. By this time I was coughing up blood. They admitted me, and soon the doctor took my mom and dad aside and said, "I don't think your daughter has long to live, but I'll do my best. The blood seems to be coming from her stomach as well as her lungs. If her brothers or sister want to see her again before she dies, they had better come soon." Overhearing those words didn't scare me; I only thought of Mom and Dad.

Dad drove back to Cherry Creek that night; Mom stayed by my side. By the time Dad had gotten back with the rest of the family, the Catholic priest had already given me the last rites. I was never really frightened to die.

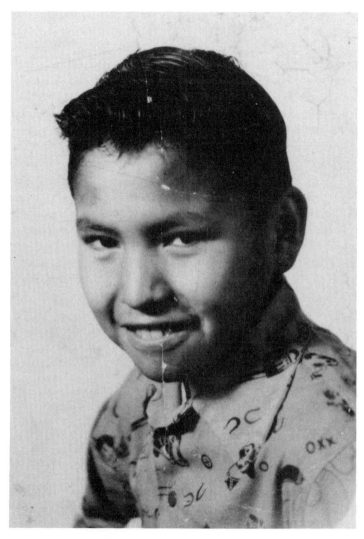

Erskin Swan, 1948.

Somehow, I knew I wouldn't die, that I would get better. Late that night the doctor gave me a shot in the back and did a bunch of tests. The next morning I felt better, and they changed my medication. The doctor looked very pleased as he checked me that morning.

He told Mom and Dad, "I think your daughter has taken a turn for the better!" Turning towards me, he said, "You have given the nurses and I a little scare! There are some people outside who want to see you." The whole family came in and wished me a happy Easter. Easter! I must have been sicker than I thought I had been, because four days had passed—precious days when I should have been home. But I thought, "We are together; it is Easter. That alone is answer to my prayers." And it was. It was still the best Easter I had seen in a long time.

They paid for all the hospital costs, my folks, and I always felt guilty about that, about being sick, even about being alive. I always seemed to be sick, so much trouble to my family. The doctor gave my parents a prescription. The pills were going to cost fifteen dollars for only ten days! Still, Mom and Dad paid for those too. Soon I went back to the san—back to life as usual, back to that place. I was glad only to see my roommates, and they were glad to see me.

Dad said, "I'll be back to see you in three months. I only hope you can come back then to stay!"

"So do I," I said hopefully, or least I tried to sound hopeful, to be hopeful.

❧   *Orby Dies: 1950*

MY BROTHER Orby had been born crippled. He had what today I would call cerebral palsy. He was a very intelligent boy, and sensitive. He kept right up in school, but he stuttered a lot. I suppose we didn't notice it as much, because he stuttered more when he spoke English at school, and we were used to it.

Orby's fingers were crippled, bent at the last joint. He couldn't straighten them. On his right hand, his thumb and index finger were permanently bent. One of his legs was also crippled, so he had a limp when he walked. He

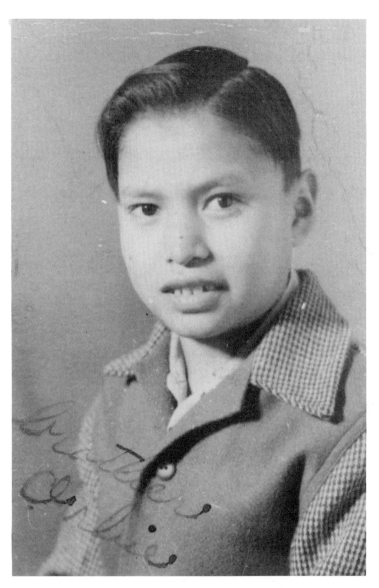

Orby Swan, 1940.

was a sweet, kind natured brother, and I cared for him very much. We all did.

When he was a student at Immaculate Conception Mission, he slid down the bannister and bruised his tail bone on the corner trim. It stayed bruised-looking there for several years; then it broke open! He grew sicker and sicker from it, and after a while he could not go to school anymore.

The folks would take him to Pierre, but they would just clean that wound out with alcohol-soaked gauze. It never did heal, though. It just stayed open like that. On one trip to Pierre the doctor did some tests. When he was finished, he told Mom, "That sore is tubercular. Orby should be in a sanitarium where they can give him better care."[16] He didn't want to leave Mom, and she did not want him to be sent away. She took him home and took good care of him there.

After a while that sore got worse. It got so bad Orby lost his appetite. It broke Mom's heart. Mom finally got sick that year, 1950, in March. I guess she had a very bad kidney infection, because she became really sick. Dad took her to the old agency hospital. They gave her some medicine to take, and Dad brought her home.

Orby told her, "You stay in bed and inside, and I'll take care of you. I don't want anything to happen to you." So they took care of her, but she got so sick she began to lose herself, where she was.

One day Orby said to her, "Mom, remember the time you said, before you die, the last thing you want is a cup of coffee, sweetened and with cream in it, and give it to you?"

"Yes, I do remember that," she said.

"Well, I fixed it for you, and you should drink some," Orby said to her. So she took it and drank a little sip, but she didn't want it. "You should drink it." She said she couldn't drink it and went back to sleep.

The next day Mom felt better. She was still very weak, but she sat up, went out doors to the bathroom, came back in, and lay down. The next day Orby said, "Mom, I really prayed hard for you this morning, and I thanked Jesus for bringing you back to good health. I didn't want you to die, Mom. I don't know what would happen to me if you died."

That is how those two felt about each other. Finally, Orby got so sick. Mom let the hospital car take him to the Sioux San. The doctor at the agency said Orby was infested with TB. When I saw him at the san, he was really thin. He had lost so much weight, I hardly recognized him. He was only at the san with me for about ten days.

The first thing he told me when he saw me was, "Sister, I don't want to stay here. I want to go home. I want to be with Mom and Dad. I'm not going to be like you. They're not going to keep me here and not let me go home." He said, "I know I'm going to die. I want to die at home. You call Mom and Dad and tell them." I said I would.

The only place we could call from then was the canteen. It was in the basement, and there was a phone down there. I went down there and called. I told the storekeeper I wanted to talk to my dad. The storekeeper said he would have Dad call back right away. Dad returned the call, and I told him, "Orby said he wants to go home, so I think you should come after him and just take him. I don't think he has long to live."

Dad said, "Well, we don't have any money right now. As soon as we get some gas money, we'll come up there."

In about ten days, they did come after him. They came up to visit me. It was sad. Mom asked, "Do you think we should take him home?"

"I think so; he'll be a lot happier there," I said. That is why they took him home.

Mom said to the doctors, "We are going to take him home because he will be happier at home." So they did, they just took him out against medical advice. They brought him home in the evening, on the eighth of May 1950. He died later that night.

They wouldn't let me go home for the funeral. I asked Dr. Sedlechek, and here, he said, "No, you have to stay here. You cannot go home." So I stayed. I felt really bad,

Lucy Swan mourning Orby's death, 1951.

because I wanted to go to my little brother's funeral. That was just one more reason I wanted to be free of that place so bad.

Mom really took it hard. He was kind of her favorite one. She probably felt that way because he had been home from school for three years. Three years she took care of him, and he worried about her, too. Now her sensitive, gentle Orby was gone, and I could not be with her.

                                    The Escape

"I'M NOT GOING to be like you. They're not going to keep me here and not let me go home. I know I'm going to die. I want to die at home." Orby's words haunted me. "Was I crazy for allowing them to keep me a prisoner here so long?" I thought. September, November, January: 1949 had changed to 1950, and I was still there changing beds, bathing the sick ones. In May, Orby, my little brother, had been buried, and they would not let me go to his funeral. It made me so angry! Freedom, to be free of this place no matter what, were the kinds of thoughts that filled my days.

In June I got word that my three month sputum culture was ready, and that I should check with the doctor. The same nervous knot grew in my stomach. Would I be paroled? Oh, I hope so. So many of my friends had either died or went home. The san was becoming a very lonely place for me. When I went to see Sedlechek, I told him I felt good and that I had not been home in a long time. "I feel good," I told him again, trying not to sound nervous or scared.

"No!" was the reply. "No, your tests are very bad. Your sputums are bad and your x-rays are bad! I can't let you go home because your germs are very bad."

"I want to go!" I screamed back. "You let everyone else go home!" I shouted at his wasicu [white man] face. I felt so bad that I had to leave, or he would see me cry. I wanted to die soon or go home, I resolved to myself. Even my chum Bernice would be leaving soon, and I'd be left here alone in this prison.

I just wanted to see my mother one more time, to tell her how glad I was for having a mom like her, to tell her how sorry I was for all my sickness and the suffering it had caused her. As I walked down that awful corridor, back toward my ward, Sedlechek called after me, "You know you're the one who is really in bad shape. You shouldn't even be allowed to walk around like this. I don't think you'll live three months!"

His words pierced into me like hot needles, into my heart. It was like a slap in the face that almost knocked me over. I couldn't even talk, I just collapsed into a chair in the hall. I couldn't think. My mind was swimming. My eyes filled with tears. Death! Death could have me, I thought. But not before I get home again!

I wrote a letter to my dad and mom and told them what Dr. Sedlechek had told me. I told them, "I am going to run away from the san first chance I get. I will not die here, to be placed out near that back door." If I am to die, it will be with my family. I asked Mom and Dad for thirty dollars to help me get home. I would find someone, perhaps Cousin Mary, someone to help me escape, I resolved. Two days later I got a telegram and the thirty dollars. The telegram said I was to come home at once. The next time Mary came to see me, she already knew of my intent to leave. "How are you going to do it?" she asked.

"I'll need some help. I think I'll get my things out a little at a time, so that no one notices. I've got a blue foot locker and my street clothes locked in storage. I'll have to get someone here to help. There is only one nurse that I can trust to even talk to about my plans," I told her, half whispering.

I was scared to even tell anyone what I had thought about for so long. "But how will you get that locker out of the building?" she asked.

"The same way I'm going!" I was excited now at even

the idea of actually getting free. "They leave one of the back doors unlocked. They leave it open for the ones who can go out for exercise. I'll carry that trunk down there with you. If anyone asks, I'll tell them you're helping me bring it back to the basement. Your husband can park the car near the corner around the back near the grounds building. The next time you come, I'll go with you the same way." There, I had said it. Now someone else shared my secret.

I had a good friend on the nursing staff. Her name was Gloria Traversy. I thought she would be the only one who would help me, the only one who would understand. Later that same day I asked Gloria if she would help. She sat there, quietly listening to my plan. Finally, she gave me her answer; she was always so kind.

"You know I shouldn't." I searched her eyes for an answer. "You know I shouldn't, but I will," she said. "During this week I'll get your locker and put your things from downstairs in it. Then when no one is around, I'll bring it to your room. We'll have to hide it under your bed. If I get caught, I'll be fired for sure!" she said, laughing quietly.

She touched my arm and said, "You are very brave. I can't blame you for wanting to go home, you have been here for so long." She smiled, and I turned to leave.

"Thank you. Thank you for all the kind things you have done for me," I told her, fighting back the tears. We hugged each other.

"Good," I thought. Gloria would put the foot locker under my bed, and I'd be ready for the next part of my plan. I slowly put all of my belongings in that trunk. Every time Mary would come, she would take things out, until little by little my things were out of that room. Finally everything was out, even my locker!

After temperature-taking time, I went into the bathroom and put on some street clothes. Then I put my house coat over my clothes, and then I started to walk out! At that time we wore dresses, so I could hide the fact that I was dressed under my house coat.

I walked by the nurses section, so frightened that I was

sure someone would notice me and want to talk to me, and I wouldn't be able to talk. I moved by one station after another until I reached the stairs. I went out the back door they left open for patients who could exercise. My heart was beating so fast when I reached Mary, I couldn't say anything. I just got in the car, and we were off.

Mary was looking very nervous. I said, "If they catch me now, the Rapid City police will arrest me like a common criminal. They will arrest all of us, put me back in the san, and you and your husband in jail. I have to make this try good!" We went all the way on back roads, we were so scared. The ride seemed to take hours, days.

Finally, about nine o'clock we got home. Everybody really celebrated! When I saw Mom, I cried out loud. I was so happy to see her. It was only the third time I had seen her since 1944. We cried and laughed and hugged. Soon she had shown me all the changes Manuel and Kermit had made in the country house over the years and caught me up on the news of our relatives. Mom and Dad, my aunt and uncle, my brothers Manuel and Erskin, Mary and her husband, stayed up all night. The next day Mary left for Cherry Creek, but everybody else stayed a couple of days longer.

We stayed out in the country ten days, ten of the best days I had spent in years. I would never go back again. If I died, I'd die at home. But everything felt, looked, smelled, and tasted good. I knew I wouldn't die. I felt so much stronger; I even gained some weight. But it wasn't to last. About ten days after I ran away, Bernice Long came.

"They know we're out," she said. "They are going to put red tags on our houses."

"That's all right, I'm staying out!" I said. Even as I said those words, a hot feeling came up my back, and I began to sweat.

Dr. Fleishman, the agency doctor, knew I was out. He told Dad, "Either take Madonna back to the san, or they will come and put red tags on your home, letting all your neighbors know that yours is a TB house!"

TB-ravaged Madonna in Cherry Creek, 1950, at home after escaping Sioux Sanitorium.

Dad said, "That's all right with me. I'm going to take her to the hospital in Pierre, not back to the san!" Dad knew I would not go back to the san since they had said I was going to die.

Why should I be sent back—I could die anywhere I

wanted or look for help somewhere else! June passed, and I was still free! In July Dad took me to see a doctor in Pierre.

Sanitor at Custer

MY FATHER HAD a good friend named Henry Standing Bear. He was from Pine Ridge, and he and Dad were old school friends. Henry Standing Bear had a daughter who was at Sioux San. She never got any better while she was there. So he took her out of there, and he got her into Sanitor at Custer. That was the "white" sanitorium for TB. Standing Bear's daughter was the first Indian in there, and she got well.[17]

When they told me at Sioux San, I only had three months to live and that I would never get well, Dad remembered his friend Henry. He wrote to him and asked him about Sanitor. Henry wrote back to my dad and said, "You'll have to take your daughter to a doctor for a physical examination. Tell the doctor Sanitor is where you want to take her. That is how you have to go about it."

So we did that. We went to Pierre. I went to Dr. Riggs, and here, he admitted me! They took x-rays and sputum tests and everything. I was there about a week, and one day the doctor came to my room. He said, "You definitely have to be in a sanitorium because your sputum is positive, and your lungs are pretty bad. The sooner you get to Sanitor the better off you will be. I can call over there and ask if there's room; that's usually a very busy place."

The next day Mom and Dad were with me when the doctor came in. "I've called over to Sanitor, and they have a place for your daughter." The doctor could not know how happy and sad his words had made me. He said, "I'll fill out this form. Then you take it back to your county seat and have the county judge and the state's attorney for your county sign these papers." Mom and Dad said they would have the papers signed. Then they thanked the doctor, and we left.

We left Pierre and went back to Dupree to have the papers signed. I went with Dad to Don Coleman's office. He was the state's attorney for Zieback County. We went in there, and Dad told them what we wanted.

Mr. Coleman just sat there. All the time he was reading, he was shaking his head. Then he threw the papers over to Hank Burgey, the judge. After a moment Don Coleman said, "Your daughter cannot go over there! The Sioux San is for Indians, that's where she belongs! She doesn't belong in Sanitor. That Sanitorium over there is for white people!"

Dad didn't say anything for a minute. Finally he stood up, then he really cursed them out. He said, "God damn you white sons of bitches! Why in hell didn't you tell us that when World War II came along? Why didn't you tell us then, that was just a "white man's" war? Many of them "Indians" didn't come home! Many of those "Indian" boys died! I had two boys that served this country, and one of them is dead. So we could have freedom of speech, freedom of religion, and freedom to live our lives the way we want to! You can't tell me I can't take my daughter over there! If you won't sign these papers, I'll go back to Pierre and tell the doctor! We'll see who's the fool!" So we came out of there.

That really broke my heart, that I had to put my dad through all this—those men who just shouted at him. When we came out, I said to him, "Dad, let's just let it go. That's all right if I die. I'm home now, that's where I want to be."

He said, "They are not going to stop us! We're going to go on! I'm going to go downtown, and if I can borrow twenty dollars for gas money, we'll turn around and go right back to Pierre." I don't know where he got the twenty, but he got it.

We bought some lunch, turned around, and headed back to Pierre. Instead of going back to the doctor's office, we headed straight for the state capitol. We went up to

Governor Sigurd Anderson's office.[18] We had to wait until he could see us, but we finally got to see him. Dad explained to him the problem we were having. He showed the papers to Mr. Anderson.

The governor said, "Well, Mr. Swan, there is no problem here. I'll sign them. I'll call Dr. Meyers first and see if there is room. Then I'll sign it." He called Dr. Meyers. When he got off the phone, he said, "If you can go over there by the seventh of September, you will have a bed." He signed the papers and repeated with a smile, "Now, you get over there by the seventh of September."

Dad smiled and said, "Thank you, sir!" The governor shook our hands.

So we came home. I got ready to go, and early on the sixth of September, 1950, we left Cherry Creek for Cousin Mary's house. We stayed at Mary's house one night, and the next day Mom and Dad took me to Sanitor.

The grounds were pretty, with trees and flowers and all. The patients were walking the grounds with their own clothes on. I was admitted. Right away they started taking tests, x-rays, and everything. That afternoon Dr. Meyers came to see me for the first time. He didn't wear a mask, and he sat down right beside me! He put his arm on my shoulder and said softly, "Your lungs are very bad, and your sputum is highly positive, according to these reports Dr. Riggs sent over."

"Regardless, I'm going to do everything in my power to help your daughter," he said, looking up at Mom and Dad.

"I'll tell you what I'm going to do. First, I'm going to inject air into her abdomen, just to try and kill that germ. If that doesn't work, I'll inject air in behind her bad lung and try to collapse it. This might kill the tuberculosis, because it needs air to grow.

"If that doesn't work, we'll have to sever the phrenic nerve. If that doesn't work, I don't know what I'll do, but I'll do something!" he laughed. Then he said, "What I want you to do, Donna, is to help me all you can. Think positive about getting well. Pray with all your heart that you will get well. You must believe it. To start with, we're going to fatten you up a little bit. I'll have the nurses put you on a special diet."

He stood up, and Dad and Mom shook his hand.[19] They were smiling. After Mom and Dad left, I lay there on the bed. I remembered living with Grandpa Puts On His Shoes. Grandpa was really a genuine good man, the kind of man that offered to my Dad his house and his land. Grandpa had told us never to trust a white man. "They'll stab you in the back!" he would say.

I had always been down on white people, but this Dr. Meyers, he sat down on the bed next to me. He touched me and spoke to me like my Dad would, just like he was an Indian or I was a white or something. I began to feel hopeful for the first time in years.

 The Treatment with Air

I WAS ORDERED to get bed rest and plenty of milk and food. That was about it for a while. Dr. Meyers would come in, sit down, and listen to my lungs. He would always take time to visit with me. In a few weeks they started to treat me by putting air into my abdomen. It was very uncomfortable, so I hoped it would work. In a few weeks Dr. Meyers told me that it wasn't working. He said, "This isn't working, so we are going to try putting air into your back and collapse your bad lung." So they did that, and it didn't work. Those days were so painful.

One day the doctor came in and said that the tests showed that the collapsed lung was still very bad. "We are going to operate and do what we call a phrenic. It will collapse your bad lung completely. I hope it works, because the procedure cannot be reversed. You will have only one lung the rest of your life, but you can still live quite normally. I hope this kills the germ."

They operated on me. A few weeks later I was told that

this had still not killed the germ enough for me to be treated with drugs. Dr. Meyers came in one day a few weeks after the surgery. He put his hand on mine and said, "Madonna, I'm sorry to tell you that our operation has not done the job. Your tuberculosis is as tough as you are."

He tried to smile. "I made a promise to you and your parents, and you made a promise to me. I'm going to a big tuberculosis conference in New York City.[20] I may learn something new that will help you. So keep being hopeful. Keep praying to get well."

I tried to be hopeful, but it was very hard. Somehow I believed this white man. I think it was Dr. Meyers and the patients at Sanitor who taught me not to be prejudiced, that there were good white people as well as bad.

Dr. Meyers

DR. MEYERS WENT to New York City to the tuberculosis conference, and when he got back, he came to me and said, "I found out something at the conference, something to try with you next. It's a procedure that has never been done in the United States before, but if you want, I will try it on you. There are five candidates here right now like you that I can try it on."

There were two women and three men. I was the only Indian. So I said, "Well, anything you want to try! I'll die if we don't do something."

Dr. Meyers said, "Well, first you must gain some weight. The surgery will be very hard on you. We are going to put you on a special diet again and see if we can't put a little weight on you."

It didn't seem as if Dr. Meyers cared if he caught TB. He would sit near us, talk with us with no mask, even if we were highly positive. He even teased us by eating food right off our tray. He was really a good man.

I had a roommate whose name was Rose Holter. She

was a high school teacher from Canton, South Dakota. She was really prejudiced against Indians. For weeks she had told the nurses, "Get that goddamned dirty Indian out of this room!" She would never look at me. I think she was ashamed to be sick and have to be in the same place with an Indian, because when her husband would come to visit, she would not let him in. "You stay out!" she'd scream. "I don't want you to see me like this!"

One day Dr. Meyers came in, and she told him, "You get that goddamned dirty Indian out of my room, or get me a new room!"

"What goddamned dirty Indian? You mean Donna here? Why, Madonna is a real good kid. In fact, she's probably a better person than you are. I don't see her screaming around about getting you out of here. You've been making trouble for her for weeks. You better understand something—tuberculosis is what you have, just like Madonna. That makes you sisters no matter what your skin color is! There is a lady upstairs who told me she would love to have Madonna for a roommate, so we're moving her this afternoon."

So they moved me. My new roommate's name was Anna Hanson. We got along swell. I think eventually Rose must have thought about what Dr. Meyers had said, because one day she asked to speak with me.

I was collecting and delivering mail to the patients who were too sick to do it for themselves. I liked doing that, because it helped me to get to know them and kept me occupied. Well, one day this Rose Holter called to me as I went by. I used to avoid her room because of the things she had said.

"Would you stop a minute or two? I'd like to talk with you. I want to apologize to you for the way I was toward you when I first came in here. I'm sorry about that. I can see that you have a lot of friends in here."

I didn't say anything. I just listened. Pretty soon she said, "Are you going to forgive me?" Still, I could not bring myself to answer her.

When I saw my roommate, Anna, I asked her, "Is that the way school teachers are supposed to act?"

She said, "No, Madonna, but sometimes people, even teachers, have to grow out of their prejudices. Maybe knowing you has helped her do that." After that, I used to pick up Rose's mail, but I didn't talk to her unless I had to.

Anna was a fine person, and she was doing real well. Anna had been doing real well. They let her get up and around and take her meals in the cafeteria. That's where she died. She was supposed to be going home, and then one day she just died. I had never experienced people dying from anything but TB, and she had died instantly of a heart attack. I just didn't know what to think. I couldn't understand how things could happen so fast.

It seemed that death followed me even in this white sanitorium where I thought miracles took place. I was kind of down about that, but my next roommate, Olga Huff, told me, "Madonna, you've been through a lot, but you can't feel like you bring bad luck. Maybe you even helped her last days to be happier. You should try to look at it that way." So I did.

❧   *Rubber Mouse*

I TRIED TO make myself useful in those days when I was getting "fattened up" for my surgery. Olga and I roomed with a lady from Sioux Falls named Fern Gorlitz. She was a doctor's wife. She was a nice little old lady, and I liked her. In fact, I liked most of the people at the san. Because I was up and around, I tried to do things for them. I had a friend who was working as a receptionist. She wasn't a patient, and she had a car. I had gotten a driver's license, and she would let me borrow her car anytime I wanted.

Sometimes I would go grocery shopping for them, get them little things that made their lives a little better. Sometimes they would even order a meal, just to try something besides hospital food, and I would fetch it for them. They liked steak and chicken, so I'd bring it back for them.

I started doing a few of the women's hair. I'd set it and comb it out. After a while I had a little business going. I never charged them a set fee, just what they thought they wanted to give me. Sometimes I got a dollar, sometimes two. The most I ever got was three. It got so I had an appointment everyday. Saturdays I'd have as many as three or four appointments. It even got so I was brave enough to cut hair.

There was this one lady named Verna who was really afraid of mice. One day somebody gave me a rubber mouse. I was fixing her hair, and about the time I was through I set that rubber mouse on her table. "Verna! Look!" I said, pointing to that mouse.

She looked at it, and her face got just white, and she screamed, "Take it away! Take it away!"

Later, I was sorry I did [it]. Verna almost died. She was really white anyway, but when she saw that mouse, she had gotten even whiter!

 "I Think You're Ready"

DR. MEYERS CAME IN one day and said I would be ready for surgery soon. He said, "We will remove some ribs and take out the upper lobe of your lung, the upper lobe of your bad left lung. Then in two weeks we'll take out the lower lobe of your lung. I hope this will enable us to use antibiotics to cure your better lung.[21] But there are risks. You may not live through the surgery. Taking out your lung may not help. I'll want to talk to your folks first."

I wrote to my Dad and Mom and told them what Dr. Meyers had said to me. Dad wrote back and said they would be right out. When he came, he brought my mom. He always took Mom along then. I told Dad, "I'm going through surgery, and I want to know what you think."

Dad said, "You are over eighteen years old. You must make up your own mind. Whatever you decide, whatever you think is best, will be all right with us."

But then he said, "If you took this surgery, and if you don't make it, if you don't come through, you would still be doing something for humanity.[22] They would learn something from this surgery. Then they can help others. The doctor told me there is a fifty-fifty chance." Dad said this, trying to hold back his tears.

After Dr. Meyers had first told me about the surgery, I felt very bad. I almost decided not to go through with it. After my dad said that, then I thought about it. Mom spoke to me; she said, "You must be brave. It is hard to be brave, and you have been very brave. Being brave does not just mean going to war and being a warrior with a gun or a bow. I told you about your Grandpa High Pine, about his kind of bravery at the Battle of The Little Big Horn. Do you remember that story?"

"Of course I do, but would you tell me again, like you did when I was a little girl?"

"Sure, I would be glad to, if you want." She began.

                        Marriage at the Big Horn

"WHEN MY MOTHER and father took each other as husband and wife, the people were camped at the Big Horn River. The people had gathered to sun dance, make marriages, take new relatives, and talk about the white soldiers and how they were trying to make them go to the reservations. There had been many reports about soldiers coming to take the people back to the agencies. There was a lot of talk about not going in, about fighting, about all those kinds of things.

"My father, Thomas High Pine, had lost his first wife some time before that, and he was alone. I think he was thirty-six years old, and Grandma Julia was sixteen. Her name was Brave Eagle Woman. In those days they didn't have names like Thomas or Julia. Those names were given to them later when they were enrolled at the Rosebud agency.

"My mother, your Grandmother Julia, was an Oglala, and your grandfather, a Two Kettle. How they came to be enrolled at Rosebud is because they were living near White River when they had the tribal membership rolls made.

"They were camped at the Big Horn, and Mom's brothers were given blankets and horses and things like that by High Pine. They were pleased that an older, settled man was interested in their sister. So they gave her to him. They took each other as man and wife in that camp about two weeks before the Battle of The Little Big Horn.

"No one knew exactly when the white soldiers would come, so it was a surprise when they attacked. There was a lot of excitement—soldiers and gun shots everywhere! My dad got on his horse, and that was the last they saw of him. There was a big fight with guns shooting all afternoon. About an hour after the first fighting started, it started quieting down some.

"They started to bring the dead and wounded back into camp, and there were so many! Mom said, 'Almost every family was in mourning.' In those times, people would cut their wrists and cut their hair for mourning.

"About two hours after the fighting, my dad was still not back. My mother and her family were very scared for him. After a while his horse came back into camp without him. Someone brought it over to their tipi. They thought for sure High Pine had been killed and that was why his horse came back without him.

"They cut off all their hair and slashed their wrists and started making the mourning sound. Mom had long braids that time, and she cut them off. All over the camp there was the awful crying of widows and mothers, and the cries of men and boys dying.

"In a while my father limped into camp on foot. When Mom saw him, she was really surprised! Then she sort of got mad at him because she and her mom had cut their hair and gashed their wrists, and here he was, alive!

"He told them that he had seen soldiers shooting women and children towards the end of the camp, so he started pulling children onto his horse and then taking them to a safe place. He kept doing that, taking women and children to a high hill away from the camp, when his horse threw him. He had badly broken his ankle. I guess it was really hurt, because it took him a while to make it back to camp. His horse was frightened, so it ran off, and he had to walk.

"So your grandfather wasn't a big hero, you know—the one that killed Custer, or anything like that. But he saved many lives.[23] That was a brave thing to do, and the families of those people he saved were grateful. So you see, Madonna, your bravery is important. You don't have to fight or kill someone to be a brave Indian. You can be brave, and they will learn something from you that will help others." Then Mom began to cry.

Later, I went to find Dr. Meyers and told him I would go through with the surgery. He said, "Your mom and dad will be right there with you if they want. I'll be doing a local, so you'll be able to see them there."

                                                      The Surgery

MOM AND DAD said they would be right there with me. On the nineteenth of February 1951 I had my first surgery.[24] Mom and Dad were there, but when they started to cut, Dad couldn't take it, so he left. Mom stayed with me, by the operating table. All she did was pray and wipe my forehead softly with her hand. A Sister was also there, and the two of them prayed for me. "Mi cinksi, mi cinksi, I'm still here," she kept saying over and over.

I was awake for the surgery. I think they must have

used some kind of Novocaine. First they had removed most of my ribs on my left side and then part of the lung. Then they sewed me back up. I had gone into the operating room at eight o'clock, and I came out at four. I was exhausted.

Two weeks later I was back down to 78 pounds, and they did it all again. I had recuperated enough. This time they took out the lower part of my lung. During the time of the surgeries I never felt sorry for myself. I was just thankful that I had gotten a chance, that I might finally get well. I tried to think that maybe someday I would once again be up and around.

                                        Waiting to Die

FOR SIX MONTHS after the surgery I was bedridden. The doctors had taken all my ribs out on one side, so I didn't have any support for my spine or head. I couldn't sit up because I didn't have any control of my head. My neck and left arm were completely paralyzed. All I did was lay in bed, and they would crank me up. I was numb from my fingertip to my shoulder all this time.

The hospital sent me to see a bone specialist in Hot Springs, South Dakota. I asked him if there were any surgery that might help me. "No, we don't want to do any more surgery. There is nothing we can do now to give support on the side where the ribs were removed, but we can build you a brace. I believe that you will eventually be able to move your head and perhaps your arm." I was fitted for a brace, put back in the ambulance, and taken back to Sanitor.

Every once in a while the nurses would put that brace on and sit me up, but my head would just flop around. Next they tied some bars above my bed so I could pull up onto that and work my head. They also gave me a rubber ball so I could work my hand. It was rough during those months after the surgery. I couldn't eat anything but a soft diet. All I had was egg nog and soft boiled eggs, Jello, things like that. During this time I felt very down; I wanted to die. I couldn't move, and I didn't seem to improve.

I told Dr. Meyers, "If I'm going to be this way the rest of my life, then it's no use. I don't want to live anymore."

He tried to comfort me and said, "You've got two good legs, and your good right arm, if you just don't give up. I have seen people worse off than you, and they didn't give up. Just keep working on your therapy, and we'll help you all we can. You will use your arm again."

I didn't listen to him; I just gave up. He didn't know how long I had suffered, with people telling me not to give up all that time. It seemed that nobody knew why I was so discouraged. I thought, "What is the use of praying and all this hope stuff." I just stopped everything, even going to church.

I told the Catholic priest I didn't want to receive communion any more. "Don't come and pray with me any more, either. Prayers aren't doing me any good. Look at me right now! I can't even help myself! I don't want to be this way the rest of my life. I've been a burden already, to everyone, so I'd rather die!" Father shook his head and left.

I stopped taking food and just waited and hoped to die. I hadn't eaten anything for about two weeks, when this Baptist minister came to my room one evening with his wife. He used to visit me now and then, and he was a good man; but I had told him not to come any more, because I was not praying to live any more.

They started to talk to me: "Madonna, these things start healing from way down in your body. It starts healing and gradually comes up to where you will feel it. You give it time, and one day you're going to get well. One day you'll be able to use your hand and neck. Make it your goal that you want to get well. God is still listening to you. You're unfinished business. He has his way of listening."

I was in no mood to listen. I had suffered for years,

not just a few weeks or months. I said, "Well, I'll think about it."

I continued to refuse food. In a few days Father Thompson came in and said, "So, what? Did you quit on us, or are you going to come back to the living?" He had a funny sense of humor and would always tease me.

I looked up at him and finally said, "I don't think I'm going to give up just yet."

Mary, my cousin, was living in Hot Springs at that time, and she would come and work on me. I had given up, but the important people in my life had not given up. Maybe that is what helped to turn me around.

One day I was lying in bed, reading. The nurses had rigged up a stand so that I could read. They fixed it so I could reach it with my good right arm. I was reading, and here the book fell off to my right side, and I couldn't get it. I had a pillow propped under my head on the right side. Every time I tried to move, the pillow would slip a little.

Finally the pillow slipped out from under my head completely. I couldn't pull my head back, so I was lying there with my head half off the bed. I was trying to push my head with my left shoulder, pulling hard as I could, first with one shoulder, then the other. Finally, I got my head back on the bed.

Slowly I moved my head over to the right, still looking for that book. Something in my neck popped. It really hurt. It just popped! I was lying there with my head facing the right. I tried to turn my head to the left. Slowly, it took all my strength, and here something popped again. I did it a few times, but it would really hurt my neck. I did it a few times that day.

The next day I worked at it again, and here, one day I moved my head slowly, very slowly, but without using my shoulder! "I did it by myself," I thought. I tried it again, and I did it. Again! Gee, I was really happy. "Olga! Olga!" I called. "I can do something!"[25] I almost screamed with joy.

"What can you do?" Olga asked, sounding amused.

I said, "Watch me!" I moved my head slowly over towards the right. I said, "Watch. I can get my head back to the left without having to use my shoulders!"

Olga got up, and she was watching me. I did it again; slowly, I moved it. Each time I did that something would pop. Olga went to tell the nurses. The nurse came in and said she wanted to watch. So I did it for her. The next day Dr. Meyers came in.

"I heard you have learned a new trick! I want to see it," he said, smiling real wide. I moved my head over one way and then back the other way. I could see by his face that he was really glad for me. He said, "I knew you could do it— I knew you would do it!"

The following day Dr. Meyers came in and said, "I think we'll take you back to the bone specialist in Hot Springs." We went over there, and he examined me. He was very pleased.

"I wouldn't be at all surprised if your left arm starts coming back too. Dr. Meyers, here, tells me that your TB seems to be improved greatly. You must be pleased."

"Oh, I am!" I said. They fit me with a new brace that had less neck support, and we went back to Sanitor.

After that, I would use my right hand to move my left hand up. It was still numb. I would try to do things with my left hand. One day I put my hair brush in my left hand. I held it and lifted my arm with my right arm. I did it day after day. Finally, one day I could hold the brush and lift my left arm to my head. It was very shaky, but I was doing it!

I kept practicing with that numb left arm and squeezing the rubber ball, and one day I realized that I could do quite a few things with it. The numb feeling slowly left my fingertips and up my arm. It wasn't until 1960 that I could feel sensations in the upper part of my arm. Dr. Meyers explained to me some time later that he might accidentally have cut some muscles or damaged a nerve.

Dr. Meyers said, "Your spine is going to be curved because you don't have any support on that side. I'm very sorry for that, but you are alive and getting better. We are so grateful for what we learned from your surgery! You were the first brave one. We are already making many changes in our technique because of you and those other brave ones who went first."

I felt embarrassed by what he had said, but I was getting better everyday. They had put me on antituberculin medicine, and for the first time since 1944 I knew I would be cured. I would live! I used to wonder why I got well, and so many others died. Maybe it had to do with what that Baptist minister had said about "unfinished business." I had put my folks through so much in the ten years I had been in Sioux San and Sanitor. I prayed to God that I would get well so that I could do something for Mom and Dad—take care of them for a change. I'd pray that for all the time and money they'd spent on me that I could repay them. I believe God heard those prayers. I believe it was because of God that I lived.

 Recovery at Sanitor

I WAS FEELING better every day. While I was still bedridden, I decided to do something besides just lie there. I enrolled in a jewelry repair class. I did most of my reading in bed. When I got up and around, I would go to the classroom to practice repair work and go over what I had learned in the books.

When I was able to get around during the two years that I was studying to be a horologist, I did a lot of things. The course went on until June 8, 1953, graduation day. There were eight of us who graduated together. I liked many of the people at Sanitor, and they liked me.

I delivered and picked up mail for the patients who could not do these things for themselves. I could leave and

Sanitor, South Dakota, public sanitorium as it appeared in early 1950.

Horology class graduation, June 8, 1953.

go to town and do shopping for them. I still fixed hair for some of the ladies, and I made a little money doing that. I knew a lot of people and had many friends. I think that whole experience gave me a good start in life. I could certainly talk and work as an equal with white people. Sanitor did this for me. They encouraged me, we encouraged each other.

Part Three

Cante᾽ ma Waste᾽ na iśtá myiyaŋpi
(Tears and Joy)

I FINISHED my studies on June 8. I was given a job as a receptionist at the sanitorium. I worked there from June of 1953 until May 19, 1954. When I got my first real check, it was like a dream come true. The check was for only $204, so I sent most of it to the folks because my room and meals were paid for. The next check I got, I asked them to come down to Custer, so they did. My dad always wore those split-leather high-topped shoes, so I bought him a new pair of those and some new bib overalls and some shirts. I bought mom and Erskin clothes, and it made me feel good.

That June I was supposed to get certified as an horologist. If I was to get licensed to work in any other state in the country, I had to serve an internship out of state. From May 1954 through July I worked in Newcastle, Wyoming, at a jewelry store. I liked it there and wished I could have stayed. The man I worked for was elderly and planned to close his shop. Soon there would be no work there, so I went back for a checkup at Custer, then on to Rapid City to live with a cousin. I worked in a café, and it was okay if you had a nice cook and if it wasn't too busy. For a while I had a real crabby cook who was very forgetful! Then it wasn't much fun. I worked there from July of 1954 until October.

I had two jobs, actually. I would work in the cafeteria from six in the morning until two o'clock; then from three till five I worked downtown for a guy who ran a drugstore. He repaired watches and clocks, and he could never get caught up, so he hired me to repair clocks. I'd go down and repair clocks and still get off by five with everyone else. That's how I earned my money. The man at Lewis's Everyday Shop offered me a full-time job, but I didn't take it because I didn't like him.

Madonna working as a receptionist at Sanitorium in 1953.

Things in the outside world didn't always prove to be so easy. My job at the drug store was to repair clocks, but eventually he had me repairing watches too. He was a man named Edward Lewis, and he made me feel uncomfortable. He never actually tried anything, but he was always trying to get close to me.

This went on for some time until one day in late October of 1954, Mrs. Lewis took the day off. We had to hang our coats and purses downstairs because that's where the cloakroom was. That day I was getting ready to leave, and Mr. Lewis followed me down the stairs. He said, "I forgot something down here." I didn't think much of it. I guess I trusted him because he had said things but never tried anything. I fetched my jacket and purse. When I had reached the stairs, he grabbed me and pulled me back.

I hung on to the railing, and I said, "Leave me alone! What the hell is going on here?!"

He didn't let me go, and he said, "I know a lot of Indian girls . . . "

I didn't let him finish; I just turned and kicked him where it hurts men the most. I said, "Well, this is one Indian girl you're not getting to know!" It must have hurt, because he fell back and let me go. I almost got to the top of the stairs when he caught me again. I had my jacket on, so he grabbed my jacket, and he pulled it off. I said, "You can have my jacket!" But I still had my purse, so I got away and ran out of there into the street. Oh, I was lucky. I never went back.

I didn't think to call the police, I just ran up the street and got a cab and went home.[1] The next day I didn't go to work; so Mrs. Lewis called, and I told her, "I quit; I'll just sign my Job Rehab papers and pick up my check." Later that afternoon I went down there. Mr. Lewis was there, but he didn't greet me. He just turned and went the other way. I told Mrs. Lewis, "I don't want to work here any more. I've already found another job, and I'm leaving. My mind is made up."

"Oh, that's too bad. We really like you here. Your work was so good, and customers like you, and. . . ."

Well, she went on like that for some time, trying to convince me. I felt bad, because I really liked Mrs. Lewis. I should have told her why I was leaving. What he did made me feel so ashamed I couldn't tell anybody. It was after that I took the job in Lead, South Dakota.

I still had to return occasionally to Sanitor for x-rays, and they would send me a little glass cup to spit in for sputum tests. They were always negative. What a good feeling getting those negative readings!

In October of 1954 Cordelia Sherilin came to visit me. She was Director of Rehabilitation from the state capital in Pierre. We got along real well; I liked her and felt she was a really grand person. She didn't like to see me working in the cafeteria. She thought it was too strenuous for me. Cordelia told me I should find something to use my mind—perhaps that I should go to college!

She wrote to me and said there was a job available in Lead, South Dakota. She said, "If you don't want this job, I think you should try college." She had already looked into school for me at Black Hills State College, in Spearfish, South Dakota. I hadn't finished high school, so I would have to finish my high school work and go to college at the same time. She had set it up for me and Minerva Little Elk, another girl from home. In October I took the job in Lead working for Mrs. Edna Heckler. She had a jewelry store and watch-repair business. I liked her and enjoyed being there, so I decided not to go to school in December.

By January 1955 I would even clerk a little once in a while. There were two of us working for Edna, myself and a man named Red Paterson. We would repair watches, clocks, and jewelry, set stones, and put birthstones on Black Hills gold jewelry, things like that. On days when Mrs. Heckler wasn't at the shop, we took turns clerking. The people in Lead treated me real well, and I liked it there. I was close enough to home that I could see my family when I wanted to or could get a ride. There were no more walls, no more disease to keep me locked in.

Dad's Strange Passing: 1953

I THINK DAD was living with someone else at this time, because he seldom came home any more. I missed him when I would go home on leave from Sanitor, and he wasn't there.

In better times, we would all sit down for Sunday dinner. Dad would talk to us on Sundays. He would read from the Bible and Grandma High Pine would pray with her pipe. Dad would pick out a scripture and relate the story to our modern situation to teach us a lesson. But these days were gone. Now there was no family to go home to like before. Mom seemed different and older.

One day I got a call from cousin Mary. She was calling Sanitor from the Old Agency hospital, and she said, "Your dad is very sick. You should come home and be with him. He's asking for you." I was in Sanitor then, but doing well, so they gave me five days off. I couldn't figure out why Dad was in the hospital alone. I thought, Mom should be there with him.

I arrived at the Agency Hospital on a Wednesday morning.[2] I stayed one night and one day with Dad, and still Mom had not called! "Four days since I got that call from Mary, and still she had not called," I thought.

By Saturday it seemed he was doing better, so I called Mom at the store in Cherry Creek. She came over to the store and returned my call. "Dad is doing better. The doctors say he will probably get better. I'm going to stay until he comes out of it," I said.

"Good," was all that Mom said.

"Why don't you come and see him?" I pleaded, but

she did not respond. Dad died the following Sunday without seeing Mom again. It was very hard for me to see him die like this, alone, without Lucy. Mom came to the Old Agency hospital the day he died. She never said very much about anything that day.

We drove the body by team and wagon to Gettysburg and bought a nice casket for Dad. All the way back to the Old Agency hospital by wagon, we hardly spoke. I didn't know what to say to her. When we got back near Old Agency hospital, all Mom said was, "I'll drive the team back to Cherry Creek and get the house ready for the funeral and wake. You can come back with one of the relatives."

When the undertaker brought Dad's body back to Cherry Creek, we had the wake, funeral, and give-away. It was tough on us, but also on Mom. Things had not been good between Dad and Mom for quite some time. Mom cried for him at the wake, but it was not until a few years later that she resolved her hurt and was able to forgive him.

Lucy and Erskin Swan on a trip to Black Hills in early 1950s.

Then she missed him, and she spoke of him often, but only in her most private moments. She told me of his drinking, of his girlfriends, of his hitting her. I began to understand her better then and why she had not felt like coming to his bedside when he was dying. I've always felt bad for that, for both of them.

Jay Abdalla

I HAD GOTTEN engaged to Jay Abdalla, I guess in 1948. He was a half-breed from Wagner, the Yankton Sioux Reservation. His mother was a full blood, his father was from Syria, I think. He came here as a boy. Jay was a buddy of Kermit's in the war. Anyway, Levi was dead by then, so I accepted Jay's ring.

Once in a while Jay would come to visit me at the san or write a letter, but that was about the extent of it. When my father died on September 20, 1953, he came down for the funeral. So I saw him; then I went back to Sanitor at Custer. In February of 1956 we got married. I was living in Lead at that time, working at jewelry repair.

I didn't know then that I couldn't have children, or maybe I wouldn't have gotten married. It wasn't until years later that a Dr. Praeger told me I couldn't have any children. He said it was all the medicine and drugs I had taken when I had TB.

Jay lived with me for a while in Lead; then he got a job working for a Mr. Butler in Faith, so that is where he stayed. He'd just come see me on weekends. Then in the fall of 1956 I came back to the reservation.

I thought the reservation had a better future for me, so I came back. I didn't find work at first. When we came home, we moved out to Manuel's place, and we took care of his cattle for him. We lived in a little cabin just ten feet by ten feet, I think.

My sister Shirley had a little boy about that time—
Austin Paul. It was soon after that, 1957 I think, Austin
was about nine months old, and he came to live with us in
that tiny cabin.[3] He called us Mom and Dad when he learned
to talk.

Austin Paul Keith, 1963.

Alta Keith, 1953.

꧁   *Austin Paul*

M<small>Y SISTER SHIRLEY</small> had a baby boy in 1956, and Mom named him. She said, "I want to call him Austin Paul. I want to do this because my son Austin Paul died so young. I loved him very much, and I want to do the things for this boy that I would have done for my son if he had lived."

Shirley and her husband were having some troubles at that time, so Austin came to live with us in January of 1957. Prior to that he would stay with us a few days at a time, but in January he came to stay with us all the time.

We lived in a tiny cabin on Manuel's ranch, eight miles west of Cherry Creek. Jay and I were caring for my brother Manuel's cattle. He paid us twenty-five dollars a month. We lived on that twenty-five dollars plus whatever game Jay could bring in. He'd bring home a deer, antelope, rabbit, grouse, or whatever! We had some commodity food, but it was hard, real hard, to make ends meet.[4] Our clothes were mostly all homemade by Mom and I, so the first clothes Austin wore with us were all homemade. The house was tiny, and we barely had room for Austin.

That spring the calves were coming before the weather warmed; we had Jay, Austin Paul, and I, plus wet, cold calves to care for in that tiny cabin. I think all we lost that year, out of thirty or more head, was two. Jay was so good with the calves and cows. We worked hard to keep Manuel's tiny herd well that spring, but Manuel said he couldn't pay any more than the twenty-five a month. So we started looking for something else. We had Austin now, and I wanted him to have the things he needed.

꧁   *Bob Samuelson's Place*

I<small>N LATE MARCH</small> of 1957 Jay got a job building stock water dams for different ranchers. He would leave for work, and sometimes we wouldn't see him for three or four days at a time. When Jay would come home, he would always chop firewood, haul water, or take care of whatever other necessities he could.

Jay was very stern with his discipline of Austin. Sometimes I think back about how I always felt when Jay was too hard on Austin. I would tell him not to be so hard on the boy. But now I'm glad that he did do that, because that helped him grow into a good young man.

In spite of Jay's disciplining, why, he was always happy to see Jay come home. He'd always look out of the window to see when Jay was coming. He was about four years old when he'd say, "Uncle Jay coming home," and then he'd watch for the tractor Jay drove back and forth from work. He was so happy to see Jay come home he'd shout with joy and run around in circles and dance!

In 1961, Jay got a job with the Samuelson brothers. From the old place west of Cherry Creek we moved to their ranch on Cherry Creek. We had a much nicer place on their ranch. There were many happy times. Now Austin had Jay and Bob Samuelson to pal around with. He really took after Bob and would follow him everywhere. Austin spoke mainly Lakota then, but Bob took that little guy everywhere he went.

When Austin started school, we went to stay with Mom in Cherry Creek. He went to the lower grades in Cherry Creek and spent the summer at Samuelson's place. He was a very happy little guy, easy to take care of; and we grew so attached to him. He thought we were his folks. He spoke only Lakota at home, but English seemed to come easy to him, and he always did well in school. Bob, Jay, and Austin have remained good friends to this day.

  Levi Comes to Visit: 1958

IT WAS 1958 when I moved back from the Black Hills for good. I moved back to Cherry Creek. It seemed I was always catching a cold. It was August, and I was living with Mom. Jay was staying at Manuel's place, watching his cattle. I really got sick, and one day Mom came back to the house and said, "I'm just worried about you, and I don't know what else to do for you. I think you should go to the doctor. So I called the Eagle Butte hospital, and somebody is going to come after you."

So they did. The hospital car came and took me to Eagle Butte hospital. That hospital was brand new then. They were moving the agency from where it used to be on the Cheyenne River to Eagle Butte so they could flood reservation land for the Oahe Dam. When we got to the hospital they admitted me right away. I was in a private room on the east side of the hospital. The nurses took x-rays of me, did blood tests, and everything. Finally a doctor came and said, "Do you know you are a very sick woman?

I said, "No, I didn't know that." I was so scared my TB had come back.

"Well, you are!" he said. "And we're going to have to really do something if we're going to help you get well."

So I asked, half afraid of his answer, "What's wrong with me?"

He said, "You have pneumonia in your one lung and it's really bad. We're going to put an intravenous in your arm, and we're going to run some antibiotics in there. I hope it will do the trick."

"Well, at least he didn't say anything about TB," I thought. The doctor went on and said, "We're also going to put you under an oxygen tent. It will make it easier for you to breathe." So they did. They put a plastic thing over my bed. I stayed under that for at least four days.

I could see Mom. I can just remember those days in spirit. My mom would come in, and pretty soon, it seemed, she walked out again. Then soon it seemed she would come in. I thought she was coming and going about every fifteen minutes. One day I was awake lying there when she came in, so I motioned for her to come over to me. She came over and pushed the tent up. "How come you keep going in and out?" I asked her.

"No," she said. "I just got here. I went home, and then I came back. I haven't been here since yesterday."

"Oh!" I said. "You're always coming in and out of here; I keep seeing you."

"No, that wasn't me," she said with a funny look on her face. "Well, I'm going to sit down here and be with you now. You just lay here and rest. The doctor said you are getting better."

I was laying there trying to figure out why Mom was telling me this, and I must have fallen asleep or something, because I saw Levi In The Woods come into the room. It was so real, not like a dream. He always used to wear a blue shirt with a tie and dark pants, and that's what he had on. He was standing there, just looking at me. I couldn't believe it was him. He was supposed to be dead, and yet here he was, I thought.

He said, "I come to see you." He rattled that plastic tent and smiled; then he opened it and peeked in and said, "You've been wanting this for a very long time, so we brought you one."

"So what is it?" I asked. They rattled that plastic tent again, and Levi's mother opened the tent.

She brought a bundle in and laid it right beside me, and she said, "Look at him, he's just cute!"[5] So I looked down like that, and it was a little baby boy! "Oh," I said. "You're right, I always wanted one!"

"Yes, I know," Levi said. "So we brought you one." I lay there looking down at my new baby; I was so happy.

Then I must have come to or woke up, and I looked and the baby was gone. There was nothing there! I started to cry, and I asked Mom where they took the baby. I was really crying now, and I sat up. "What baby?" Mom asked.

"Levi and Maisy!" I said.

"Nobody was in here but me—there is no baby," she said with a worried look. I got much worse after that. The next time I woke up, Father was giving me the last rites, praying over me.[6] But I did pull through. I got well. I was real weak for a long time.

"You'll have to stay in the hospital two or three weeks

until you get your strength back," the doctor said, after I was out of danger.

I couldn't stop thinking of that dream, though. It seemed so real. I wished it could have been real, but it wasn't. Levi was dead, and I was alive.

                                    "What Is a Bum?"

I TRIED, —we tried, Mom and I—to teach Austin the good things of life. He was a happy little guy and never had any bad feelings towards anyone or anything. He already had a good attitude towards life.

Once or twice Austin decided he didn't want to go to school anymore because he didn't like a certain teacher. I asked him, "Why don't you want to go to school anymore?"

He said, "Because I don't like that teacher. She's really mean! So I'm not going to school anymore!"

"Hmm! So do you want to grow up to be a bum?"

"So what's a bum?" he asked.

"Those are the ones that people see carrying a little bag on a stick, and they walk the roads," I said. "They don't have any education; they don't have any skills or anything! They keep hitchhiking all the time, and they are dirty because they only have one set of clothes! Is that what you want to be?" I asked.

Austin's eyes got real big. "Well, no!" he finally got out. He went outside and thought about it for a while. "I'll go back to school, I guess, even if the teacher is mean. I don't want to be a bum!"

Mom Remarries: 1962

MOM WENT to stay with Alta and I at Old Agency for a while after Dad's death. We lived with Mary Swan and her family. Eventually, I moved permanently back to the reservation, back to Cherry Creek and lived with Alta, Austin, and Jay. It was in 1962 that I realized the strong feelings Mom still had for Dad's memory. I came to know this in kind of an odd way.

That year Mom married Francis Straighthead. Angeline, his daughter, was married to my brother, Manuel. Old Mr. Straighthead's wife had died, so Mom went ahead and married him. They weren't married for very long when trouble broke out. Angeline and her brother were always trying to get their dad to sign or will all of his property over to the two of them. I was at Mom's house one afternoon when Angeline said to her dad, "I want you to sign them!"

Her dad protested. "You better sign them!" his son yelled. "If you know what's good for you," he shouted right in the old man's face.

Mom was getting pretty upset; tears filled her eyes. "We don't want you Swans in our will. We want you to leave your land to us and them Swans out!" they repeated to their dad, right in front of us.

I had finally had enough! "No suicide-committing son of a bitch is going to tell us Swans what to do in our own house! This is our house, Mom's house. Nobody is going to come in here and tell us what to do in our own house!" I shouted back at them.

Francis spoke up, finally responding to my words. "Well, I guess I better get out if that's the way you feel," he said, turning towards Mom.

Mom shouted at him next, "If you are going to leave here, you better take all your stuff and move out! Don't come back! I'm not fooling with you!" she shouted.

Gee! Mr. Straighthead sure caught hell from everyone that day. His ears must have been really ringing. It wasn't long afterwards that Mom had her marriage annulled. She took back her Swan name and has worn it proudly ever since. I think after that she spoke fondly of Dad more often and let people know she was proud to be Mrs. James Swan, even if their lives together had known rough times. She never met a man who could take his place beside her!

The Cattle Program

IN 1954 the Cheyenne River Sioux tribe announced a cattle program for members of the tribe. The Cattle Rehab Program, as it was called, gave each qualified applicant ten thousand dollars in cash. They also bought you a new pickup truck, new farm machinery, and one hundred head of cattle.[7] You were supposed to start a cattle ranch with that. When the first year was up, you were supposed to repay the program with so many head per year.

I applied for the program. Jay couldn't, because he was not a member of the Cheyenne River Sioux Tribe, and we weren't married yet. They told me I wasn't living on the reservation at the time, so I didn't qualify for Rehab.

Next we tried the Replacement Program. In this program you got only fifty head, no money, and no farm machinery. Participants were supposed to repay the tribe so many cattle per year. I guess we were put on a waiting list, because we never did hear about being accepted.

In 1958 Jay and I were living in the country near Cherry Creek. We were watching my brother Manuel's cattle. Austin was living with us at the time, and the house we were all living in was about ten by ten feet. It was very crowded living there. That spring we had a bad blizzard about the time Manuel's cattle were calving. So in that little house we had Jay, Austin Paul, myself, and about ten calves! Jay would go out and pick up the new born calves; then he would bring them in, and we would dry them off and feed them, to get them started. That spring we always had calves staying with us! Now, looking back, it does seem pretty funny!

All over the reservation that spring many cattle and calves died of the cold and snow, but we saved every one of Manuel's. Manuel had promised Jay half of the calves that year, but he went back on his word. This would have been the spring of 1959.

The tribe had a field agent named Joe LaPlant working

as a field supervisor. Mr. LaPlant would stop by our place, if he was on his way to Bridger, and eat lunch with us. If he was coming back through in the evening, he would often stop in.

One day he said, "I don't understand why you two don't get on one of the cattle programs."

I told him, "We tried to get on the rehab program in 1954. They said we weren't living on the reservation."

Joe said, "I'm going to look into this." Then he left.

Some time later Joe brought us an application to apply to the Replacement Cattle Program. "They give you so many head of cows; then you are to start paying back the program in calves. The first year on the program they want seven heifers. That would be your total payment on the program until next year," Joe explained.

In June or July of 1961 we started to get our cattle. By that September we had gotten all our cattle. We were supposed to get started with a small number. I think all together we got forty-one head. We were supposed to pay back seven heifers, according to Joe, but the first year we didn't have to pay back in. We were told we could skip that year and start repaying them the following year.

We had enough heifers that fall, so Jay said he was going to make the first payment anyway. He did that in the first year and every year after that. Whatever was necessary, we would always repay. I was proud of him. We had been living at Manuel's place, but Jay had taken a job with Bob Samuelson, a white rancher who lived on the reservation. Jay had an agreement with Mr. Samuelson. He worked on Bob's ranch in exchange for care of our cattle. Our cattle were running with Mr. Samuelson's. This was the kind of agreement we had. He was a genuine good person.

We didn't live in the country near Cherry Creek any more. We were living near Samuelson's place in a house he had for hired hands. It was bigger than the little cabin at Manuel's. Austin loved the place and he liked Bob Samuelson. He and Bob got to be real pals, it seemed Bob took

Austin everywhere he went. Austin really liked Jay too, so he was becoming a real little cowhand.

Life went along smoothly like this for quite a while. We had soon paid back most of the cattle we owed, about thirty head, I think. Finally, we quit Samuelson's and moved back to Manuel's place.

🌊   *Head Start Years*

IN 1966 I began to work for the Head Start Program; Austin was in school then, so it was a good opportunity.[8] Maybe because I couldn't have a bunch of kids of my own, I really enjoyed my job. There were so many things the kids did or said during those years that would make me laugh. It seemed, too, that there were always people after my job, trying to make trouble for me. Even some of those times were pretty funny.

There was this one time I had this student named Jeff Knight. He was a cute little boy and already had an interesting way of looking at the world. It seemed that spring there was a funeral every day in Cherry Creek. I guess Beatrice, the other teacher, was using the funeral processions to work with the kids on their counting.

Jeff came into my room one day and said, "Aunty Donna, there were forty-two cars going to that funeral. There were fifteen pickup trucks, and the rest were cars!" He stood there beaming, proud of his counting.

I told him, "Jeff, you shouldn't be counting those cars. I don't count funeral cars, because there's a superstition that if you count those cars, you'll be the next one to lead the procession. So we never count cars at a funeral," I said, teasing him.

"Oh, it won't be me," he said.

"That's good!" I said. So he was standing there quietly looking out the window when he asked, "Aunty, aren't you glad you're a Catholic?"

Ethel, Lucy, and Erskin Swan, 1968.

Now, that had me puzzled, but I said, "Why, yes I am."

"Cause you know why?" he asked. "It's good to be a Catholic because there's too many Episcopals dying." It seemed he was right; when I thought about it, all of the funerals that spring had been Episcopalians. I've laughed about what he said many times since.

There were these two women, Caroline White Horse and Angeline Afraid of Hawk, who wanted my job, and they were always making trouble for me. They were against me from the first day I started working for Head Start. They would say things to people like, "She shouldn't

Madonna Swan-Abdalla, 1968.

be working there—she never even had any kids of her own. She doesn't have any business working with kids." So they used to watch me.

In those days we would go to work at eight o'clock and get off at five. So they'd watch the clock every morning and make sure that I was there right at eight. Well, I lived way out in the country, and if I was late by even a few minutes, they'd mark it down on a calendar. If I was late three times they would call the program director, Mr. Olsen, in Eagle Butte and try to make trouble. That Angeline was my stepsister, because she used to be a Straighthead, and my mom was married to her dad for a short time.

Anyway, they used to watch me, and gee, they gave me a hard time. One day I got tired of them, and I went to see Mr. Olsen. I said, "If those two say I'm late all of the time, well, I could resign." He smiled and said, "No! No, Madonna, you can't be worried about them. Let me handle them. We don't have any complaint against you. Just let them dogs bark!"

Little Scholar

THERE WAS a man in Cherry Creek who came to my classroom one day upset about how I was teaching his son. His name was Clement; I think he lives in Utah now. His little boy was four years old, and he had been attending Head Start, September, October, November, and now it was December.

One day he took home some papers he had painted. Later that same afternoon his father came in, and he looked angry. He said, "Is this all that you teach these kids in here? Just to make these different painted lines on these papers?!"

I said, "Why, yes, it is one of the things we teach them in here."

"I thought maybe he'd be doing ABC's, arithmetic, and reading."

"No," I said. "He's not ready for that yet. When he goes into the other room he'll be ready for that, but right now we're just trying to help him socialize with the other kids."

"Hmm! I want him to learn to read and write and learn arithmetic," he said glaring at me.

"Oh, okay. When he goes to the other room, he will learn to do those things, but right now we're just getting him ready to do that."

But that didn't seem to satisfy him. He was going on and on about what Head Start was supposed to do, when I finally had enough, and I interrupted him. "Clement, when you were young, did you know how to read and write and do arithmetic?"

He said, "Yanketo [wait a minute], I want to think." So he was standing there, and finally he said, "Hiya, sni sle ca (No, I don't think so)."

So I said, "And yet you expect your son to do that, and he's only four years old."

"Ohon, he cetu, ce (Oh, yes, that's right, isn't it)," he said.

❦   *Brother Johnny*

CHILDREN SOMETIMES have imaginations that are amazing. One time I was talking with the children about the idea of family, about what a family was and how important each member is, things like that.

I gave the children a bunch of old magazines and told them, "Cut out pictures of people from the magazine and pretend they are members of your family. When you get them cut out, paste them on the paper and make a family like the one you live in. Make sure you have the right number of brothers and sisters. When you finish them, we'll all tell a story about our families in class."

So they were doing that, sitting down, going through the magazines, and cutting out people. "When you get finished, take the finished picture and pin them up over there," I said. In the "Indian way" I had a granddaughter in that year's class. She was my brother Manuel's grandchild, Geri Demery. When she was through with her picture, I told her to pin it up on the board with the others.

When all the children were done, I said, "Now, each of you go up to your picture and tell us all about your family. Tell us how many brothers and sisters you have and what their names are." So they were doing that, and pretty soon it was Geri's turn. "Now, Geri, you go up and tell us about your family."

She got up, and she said, "This is my dad, and this is my mom, and these two are my two brothers, and these are my two sisters. I got one big sister and one little sister."

So I laughed, and I said, "Why, Geri, you only have one brother; how come you've got two up there?"

She insisted, "No, I got two brothers!"

I asked her, "If you've got two brothers, where is the other one?"

"I don't know, but I think he's in Nashville, Tennessee," she said.

So I asked her, "What's his name, then?"

She snapped her eyes at me and said, "Johnny Cash, and he lives in Nashville!"

I had to chuckle—she even knew where her "brother" was.

The Long Trouble

IN 1969 I was working for the Head Start Program in Cherry Creek. I used to drive back and forth from the country. Jay was working for Wally Knight. We had a car and a pickup, because we went in two different directions to work.

After school one evening I stopped at the store in Cherry Creek. I stopped to get our mail and some grocer-

Madonna speaking at Head Start graduation, 1971.

ies. There were two women standing outside the Post Office, talking; when I overheard them say, "Abdalla," so I
listened. "Yes, it's true; they're going to take away Jay
Abdalla's cattle," one of them said.

The other woman asked, "Why are they doing that?"

"I don't know—they rounded them up and hauled
them over to Miner's place."

I turned around and saw that it was Rosaline and Sadie
Hale. They just looked at me and wouldn't say any more.
Instead of getting what I wanted, I just said, "Fill the tank
with gas." So I turned around and drove home to the
country place. I decided to drive past our place and look
for Jay. When I got to Miner's place, there were some cattle
in the corral. I went as far as the gate and could see that
some of them were ours!

So I turned around again and headed back towards
Cherry Creek, still looking for Jay. As I drove, I saw Jay
coming. I stopped him and told him what was going on.

He yelled, "I'll go park the pickup over to your mom's, and we'll go see about this!"

Reuben Ward was the tribal councilman from our district then. Jay said, "We'll go up to Reuben Ward's place and find out what the hell is going on!" We stopped at Mom's. Jay got in the car and drove off. Reuben Ward lived up here then, in Cherry Creek District. So we drove there, and Jay stopped in front of their door, and I went in. "Hou!" I said. "Hi!" he answered.

"What's going on? How come they're rounding up our cattle?"

"I don't know. I don't know for what reason they're doing that," he said. "But they wanted them cattle rounded up, and that's why they're doing that!"

His wife turned to me and said, "They are going to take them cattle because you aren't taking care of them. They're running all over! That's why they are going to take them!"

"That's nothing but a big lie!" I wanted to shake her.

Reuben kept saying the same old thing, "I don't know why."

"Well, who the hell knows what's going on?" I asked.

"I don't know," was all Reuben could say.

I came out and told Jay, "Reuben says he doesn't know anything!"

Jay answered, "Let's go down to Alex Chasing Hawk's—he'll know what's going on!" So we went to his place.

Alex said, "Hon! Yes! The tribal council is doing that. I tried to tell them not to do that, but they outvoted us. It was the rehab extension committee of the tribal council."

"So they are going to take our cattle. What for?" I asked.

"Oh, I don't know. They said something about Jay and your brothers Manuel and Erskin selling some calves off the reservation," Alex said.

"Who said that?" I asked.

"Well, that's what Reuben Ward reported," he said. "But you can come up tomorrow to the tribal office, and you can protest it. Don't worry, you can straighten the whole deal out."

We left there and went back to Miner's corral. Our cows were still in the corral. Jay said, "Why don't you open that gate? Just turn them out. You're a member here. They can't do this to you!" But I didn't, because I was afraid we would get into even deeper trouble. So I didn't let them out; we just let it go for the night and went home.

The next day we went to see the committee, and they accused Jay of stealing cattle! They said, "He took ten steers across the river and sold them." They accused my youngest brother, Erskin, of helping them.

"How can you prove that?" I asked.

"We got them back, that's how!" they said. They had gotten steers from Jim Hunt's place.

Jay had a good friend, Mr. Newhouse, who owned a ranch across the river. I told the rehab people, "He made a deal to take some of our cattle and fatten them over the winter in exchange for Jay working for him part time." They had just brought them over, and Mr. Newhouse changed his mind and brought them back. Mr. Newhouse loaded them up and left them at Jim Hunt's place for us to pick up. He did this because a rehab committee member went over to Mr. Newhouse's place and scared him.

Mr. Newhouse told the rehab committee men, "I was only going to feed them in exchange for work!" So then Mr. Newhouse brought them back.

We heard later that they didn't want us to know anything about any of this. They came and took them behind our back.

"Nobody stole anything from you!" was all the council committee would say, but they were stealing from us! We couldn't get anything done because they were all in on it. Eventually, they dropped the cattle rustling charges, then they said, "You broke your contract by taking the cattle over there." That was their justification!

The Cattle Rehabilitation Committee wrote us a letter not long after that. They told us that according to our contract and those of the other rehab operators, no one was supposed to move any cattle off the reservation unless they had a permit. They said it didn't matter whether we were going to sell them, or run them for feed, or whatever. That's why they were confiscated.

                                  Money or Cattle

WE TRIED to fight them, but we couldn't get anything done. They kept covering up for each other. So we went to see a Legal Aid lawyer. That spring the committee wrote to us and said they sold our cows for $135 apiece. They had sold the steers, and with the money they paid all my debts and loans at the Tribal Credit Office, which was a total of only $882. They said the rest of the money was at the tribal office. They explained that we could have the balance in money or cattle.

Time went by and nothing happened. We didn't hear anything about the money or the cattle. Soon we went to the tribal office to see Tribal Chairman Frank Ducheneaux. I went in and asked him about it. I should have taken someone in with me for a witness, but I went by myself.

Frank Ducheneaux said, "Oh, yeah, they sold your cattle, so there is about seven thousand dollars left. What do you want to do? Do you want the money or the cattle?" he asked.

Jay and I already talked it over, so I told him, "We want the cattle!"

"Okay!" Ducheneaux said, "I'll tell the committee, and whenever they have some turn-ins, they'll give you some." They figured we owned twenty-nine and a half cattle. So that is what we agreed to, but we never heard anything after that.

We decided to go back up to the extension office because we had land-lease money coming, and the tribe owed us money for the cattle we had sold. That same year we had sold some cattle at the Cheyenne River Sioux tribe sale barn and at the Faith Livestock Company. The checks for these cattle had to be sent through the tribe, I guess, so the tribe would be aware of the sale. We had never gotten the checks for those sales.[9]

At the extension office they told us those checks were around the office someplace, but they couldn't find them just then. Later, we had a meeting with the Tribal Rehab Committee. At that meeting we told them we were tired of all this business, and we would take the committee to court.

Frank Ducheneaux was at that meeting, and he said, "Madonna, if you take the tribe to court, you will lose all your rights as an Indian." He said, "You'll lose your land, your benefits from the tribe, and everything else."[10] I didn't want that to happen to me. I didn't know how to think about what Frank had said, whether this was actually possible.

We had also asked them about the money they owed us—seven thousand dollars plus cattle sale money and lease money. They told the secretary to run and get a book. So she brought it back, and the committee chairman and Frank were looking at it. It was a great big book. I don't know what was in it, because they didn't show it to us.

They held it up and were paging through it. Tuffy Ducheneaux, Frank's brother, slapped the book shut and said, "All them checks are in here. Whenever we get this straightened out, we'll return the money." So then we didn't know what to do, whether to believe them or not.

❧   *Land Grab!*

WE HAD BEEN talking about our problem with a Legal Aid lawyer named Mr. Lindquist. He started working on our case. One day he called us into the office. I think it was

June of 1971. He said, "The tribe had told me to leave the reservation because of cases like yours. So I can't pursue this for you any further. Good luck." So he left the reservation. Certain members of the tribal council ran him out. We knew that this was pretty much the end of our chances to get justice. They even took our cattle grazing units away and leased them to Maynard Dupris.

They just wanted us out. That is what started and caused the whole thing—land! Reuben Ward was the councilman; Maynard Dupris is his nephew. Millard Dupris is Reuben Ward's brother in law. They wanted us out because they wanted our unit to run cattle for white ranchers who live off the reservation. Millard and Maynard had a unit together, and it adjoined ours. He wanted this unit, too, so they moved us out. It was simple for them because he was a councilman.

It was all corrupt. They knew Jay was a nonmember and couldn't do anything. That left just me to contend with, so they ran us out. But the story isn't over. Along comes greedy Maynard, and he gets a foothold in council and kicks Millard out![11] Maynard still has those units now. He runs outside cattle from across the river for anybody and everybody, on our land! He even sells cattle off the reservation without the I.D. (reservation) brand on them. Because of underhanded things like this most of the full bloods who were on the program didn't have a chance.[12] They just went in and took them over and took over the leases on their lands.

                                              The Missing Check

ONE DAY that spring in 1971 the superintendent of the rehab. program, Justin Lawrence, stopped in to the Head Start office where I was teaching. He said, "Madonna, you got some money in the rehab. office. One of your cows died out there at the sale barn, and there was insurance on it. The check is laying around up there. I saw it. You can go up there and get it."

"I work all day at the Head Start and can't get away. Next time you come, would you bring it?" I asked.

"Okay," he said. "I'm coming down Thursday, so I'll bring it."

Thursday I saw him drive by, but he never brought the check. That Friday I got this letter, and it said, "You have five head of cows at the tribal beef camp. If you don't pick them up by five o'clock Friday, you won't get them at all!"

I told Jay, and we went up to Eagle Butte and out to the beef camp. We hired a man to take the cows back up to our place and paid him thirty dollars. When I saw the cows, I knew why we had to pick them up that day or forget it! They were starved almost to death. One of the cows was lying down, just sick and skinny! The others were really thin, too, but at least they were still on their feet!

We loaded the cattle up. Jay was really mad. He was good with cattle, and it made him real angry to see them all starved like that. What angered us even more is that those five were ours—five of the ones the tribe had taken and said were sold! At least these four or five were better than nothing. So we followed those sick cows back to Cherry Creek.

Jay started feeding them with cotton cake feed, and every morning he took the tractor and lifted the sickest cow to her feet. We gave them water and really watched them. In a week the sick old cow finally got better and could stand by herself. So she came out of it. They had simply starved them!

They had never sold our cows like they said. They lied. I think they divided them up among themselves, because we had fine cattle; most of them had been sired by a Brahman bull Jay had bought. I never did find out why they didn't feed them. So we got our five cows back, and they were actually our cows!

We couldn't get any further with the tribe. I decided

Frank was wrong about my Indian rights, and besides, he
wasn't chairman any more. I went back to Legal Aid to a
Mr. Dick Churchwell. He couldn't do anything.

The same bunch who did us in the first time still weren't
satisfied. Soon, they came and rounded up our four cows
we had left. They loaded them up to the Miner's corral without us even knowing it—after they were all fattened up.

That summer I went to the hospital in Rochester in
1971. It was getting harder and harder for me to breathe
or get around. So Jay took me over there. And while I was
in the hospital they took them. I never got paid for those
four cows, either.

Millard Dupris got paid ten dollars a piece for rounding them up! When we got back, I asked him why he did
that. He played dumb and said, "Well, the rehab. committee said to round up any cattle with the Jay brand,
so I did!"

I told him, "They gave us back those cattle—those are
ours."

But he just said, "I didn't know that," and walked away.

You see, sometimes I think it was a good thing that
I got TB and ended up at Sanitor with all those white
people. That experience taught me a lot about life. If some
of these people had ever gotten out of here, maybe they
wouldn't have the rotten attitude towards white people like
they do. They would have found out that there are good
and bad in every kind of people. They would have realized
that sometimes we Lakota are our own worst enemy.

                         Jergen's Lotion

JAY ALWAYS LIKED to drink with his buddies; white or Indian, it didn't matter. I used to wait out in the car. Austin
and I would sit there and wait, sometimes for hours. One
day, I think it was 1964, Jay stopped at the bar in Dupree
to have some drinks.

I grew tired of waiting, so finally I went in the bar to let
Jay know I wanted to get back to Cherry Creek. The bar
was L shaped, and Jay was standing near the corner of the
bar; I went and stood right beside him on his left. There
were a lot of other guys standing around, and they made
me nervous.

I was standing there, and here, this one mouthy white
man came up to me. I didn't know who he was, so I was a
little frightened of him. He said, "I'll bet you I could get
any squaw I want." And then he said something about how
he could buy a few drinks and pat them on their backsides
and "they'll be mine for the night." Things like that.

I turned away and poked Jay. I said, "Let's go. I'm tired
of this place."

"Just one more drink," Jay said. So I moved around
and stood on his right side next to a man named Leonard
Cook. He was a half-breed, but he spoke good Indian.[13] So
I got between Leonard and Jay.

I was standing there, and Leonard Cook said in Indian,
"Aw, Madonna, don't pay any attention to that guy. He's
just a big blow off." He finished in English, looking right
at the white man. The white man just walked over and pat-
ted me on the fanny. He was mumbling the same things he
was before.

He said, "Aw! These old squaws, all you have to do is
touch them in the right place, and you can have them." He
was going on like that.

Gee, I saw red! I turned around, and I just hit him on
the head with my purse and knocked him down. He was
out cold! I said all kinds of things to him, and I said a lot
of bad things, too! "No white man is ever going to touch
this 'squaw' even if some squaws are that way—this one is
not one of them, you son of a bitch! Get up and I'll knock
the hell out of you again! No white man is going to touch
me and get away with it!"

Jay sobered up in a real hurry, and he took me out of
there. When we got to the pickup, I began to wonder why
that man was knocked out so easy. I looked in my purse
and there was an unbroken bottle of Jergens lotion I had

bought that morning. I started to laugh, and Jay said, "What's so funny?"

"This! Your friend was done in by Jergen's lotion." So then we both had a good laugh. Oh, how I hated that guy after that. I never saw him for quite some time, but every time I saw him, I would turn my back.

I had a friend, her name was Mrs. Virginia Till. She was a grand lady with a hard working husband. They were a white couple just trying to get started. They moved down near Cherry Creek when they had only one child who was about nine months old. They moved down to what had been old Mr. Yellow Owl's place. We lived out in the country then, so we were neighbors. We got acquainted and hit it off right away. That summer we planted a garden together. We hauled water together and watered the garden. Whatever we got from the garden we shared. We canned together, picked wild cherries, we did all sorts of things together.[14]

By the end of the summer Mrs. Till had two children, and I helped her look after them. Austin liked their place and was always following Mr. Till around or trying to help us. It turned out that the man I had clobbered at the bar was Mrs. Till's cousin! I didn't know that, but I guess he came down to visit her one day and told her that Jay Abdalla's squaw had cold-cocked him. He was laughing about it, so Virginia really laid into him. She said, "That serves you right. She should do it again! She's a good person. She doesn't drink, and she's about the best friend I ever had!"

One day about two months after the bar incident we went to Dupree to shop. Mom, Austin, and I went into the grocery store. When we got what we could afford, we left and got back in the car. Soon Jay came down the street.

"Mr. Amundson wants to apologize, to talk to you, but he's afraid to come over," he said.

"What the hell does he want to talk about?" I asked. "Does he want another hit on the head?"

"No," Jay said. "I think he just wants to apologize. I think you should talk to him."

"No way! I'm not going to apologize to him, and if I can

help it, he's not going to get the chance to apologize to me, either!"

"I think you should at least hear this Amundson guy out," Jay said.

Mom tapped me on the shoulder from the back seat and asked in Indian, "What is Jay talking about?"

"Oh, nothing. He said some man wants to talk to me, but I don't want to talk to him!" I told her.

Soon the man was near the car. I just sat in the front passenger seat and looked the other way. He had a big cardboard box with him. It had coffee, oranges, and bread, and I don't know what all in there.

"Mrs. Abdalla?" he called softly. I got out of the car and kept my back turned. "Mrs. Abdalla, I want to apologize to you," he said. "Ginny, my cousin, told me all about you, what a help you have been to her, what a good woman you are, and I want to say I'm sorry. I would like to give you these." He held out the box.

            Austin Makes a Decision

AUSTIN HAD BEGUN to spend some time with his folks. I think he was nine or ten when he realized Jay and I were not his mother and father. By this time, Shirley and her husband, Sidney Keith, were doing much better and wanted Austin to live with them and go to school in Eagle Butte.[15]

He spent quite some time thinking about what he should do. Finally, he told us that "Even though I love you and Jay and Grandma very much, I should get to know Shirley and Sidney and my sisters better. And I heard that school in Eagle Butte is better. Try not to be sad. I'll come to see you all the time." He tried to be brave, and we tried to be brave.

He made a decision that was important, and even though it made me sad, I said, "Okay, then, you go and do real well, so we can keep being real proud of you." I hugged him and hugged him. I would miss him so.

Austin came to visit often, and he spent large parts of his summers with us. When I'd feel down, you know, he'd say, "What's the matter, Aunty Donna? Remember what you told me about being sorry for myself." And he'd kind of cheer me up with a little lecture I had once given him. It was nice to talk to him. We could and still can talk about things he doesn't share with anyone else.

Austin continued to come down to see us the whole of his young teen years. He'd share his problems or what he was thinking about. And it seemed I'd always know when he was worried about something. I'd ask him, "Son, what is it that's on your mind?"

He'd always say, "Oh. Well. No. Nothing. It'll all work out." But later he'd tell me, and so we'd talk it over and find a solution together.

 A GED Dark Horse

SOMETIMES THINGS work out in the most unusual way. We were working as teacher aids in the Head Start Program in 1967. I was supposed to take my Graduate Equivalency Diploma, but they kept postponing it because I wanted to study more. I suppose I was a little nervous about the idea.

A girl friend of mine, whom I worked with as a teacher, was also supposed to take her GED. She had an opportunity to go on a training session to Lincoln, Nebraska. She said she couldn't go because she didn't have her GED. I kept telling her, "Why didn't you go? It's really a good opportunity for you."

"But taking a GED is really hard," she would reply. Finally, when the time was getting close, I told her, "Why don't you get the books, and we'll study. We only have two weeks if you're going to make that trip!"

I told my friend, "I'll help you study, and I'll go with

you." Now I was committed to take it, too. We really studied. We'd often work till late at night. We studied every spare minute we had together. We had to go to Gettysburg on a Saturday because the trip to the training session in Lincoln was on the following Monday. So Saturday we went to Gettysburg. We both really had butterflies!

We took the test, and it took all day! We finished the test, turned around, and came home. That Monday she went in and told the supervisor that she was going because she had taken the GED. We didn't even know if we passed! They were supposed to send us a letter if we did. So we didn't know for a while if we even passed, but she went. Soon I learned that we both passed and got our GED. I was very happy for her. I suppose it was from that time in 1967 that I started taking college classes. My dream of a college education for myself was rekindled.

                                    A College Chum

ALL OF US Head Start teachers took college classes provided by Head Start here in Cherry Creek during the winter. During the summers we would go to Spearfish, to Black Hills State College. I did this until I got so sick I had to resign. That was in 1971.

In the early years of the Head Start Program you had to pay for your own college courses. Tanya Ward, another teacher's aid, and I decided to scrape together enough money to do it. So we did. Tanya was from the Red Scaffold community on our reservation. We saved up our money to take classes. We scraped up enough to go to our first summer session at Black Hills State. No one seemed to like Tanya. Reservation people in the teacher program were kind of down on the Ward family. "Why don't you like them?" I would ask different ones.

"Oh, they just act like they are too good for the rest of us people!" was the general reply.

I got to know Tanya and found out that she was a very bright and sincere person. I became good friends with her. I had gotten acquainted with Tanya doing an eight-week course at Arizona State University and found she wasn't stuck up at all. She was very funny and loved to make us laugh.

Tanya started in her education the same time I did. Now she's completing her doctorate! I'm so proud of her! I'm just really proud of her and proud to be her friend. Recently she got an award, Outstanding Educator, from the South Dakota Indian Education Association. So I tell anyone that knows her how well she has done, and some people didn't even think that it's nice—but I think it's great![16]

                    Traveling Companion

IN NOVEMBER of 1973 Jay and I had a good friend who had passed away. His name was Wally Knight. He was a good old man, a white man who had married a full-blood named Sarah In Amongst. They ranched for many years down in Red Scaffold community.

Wally was well liked by everyone because he minded his own business unless he was asked to help with something. He treated everybody well and always seemed to be doing something interesting. For some time he had been trying to raise buffalo. People liked to see his buffalo on the reservation because of what the buffalo meant to our people.

One time he had this old bull named Buster that got loose. There were rumors about that big bull from one hundred miles to the south. People had seen him clear off the reservation, down the Missouri River towards Pierre. Some months later that buffalo just came back on his own. He was real sick and scrawny and had some twenty gunshot wounds. Nobody thought he would make it, and they told Wally he should just finish it off. Well, he patiently nursed old Buster back to health, and that crazy animal lived to make more buffalos! When we'd go for a visit he'd always tease me, saying things like, "Madonna's here, so we better make her a extra big supper and try to fatten her up!"

The fall of 1973 I saw my seventh year as a Head Start teacher. I loved my work at Head Start. It was as if, despite my tuberculosis and my not being able to be a nurse, go to school, or do the things I had dreamed of, I was finally doing something that made me feel happy. Head Start had a strong staff development program that included working on a teaching degree if you wanted it. By that November I had come close to finishing my degree.

We were in Eagle Butte on a workshop. It was a strange day—kind of cloudy windy and cold. We were supposed to write some reports for college credit, dealing with our personal goals in education. They gave us six months to do them, but Chris Ellison, a non-Indian girl, and myself had finished ours and had turned them into Faye Longbrake, the new director. When we turned them in, she said, "I think you should try to help the others, since you've got yours done."

So I was going to help Rose Dupris, and Chris was going to help Victoria LeClaire. We had to write about our job in Head Start, the kind of work we do, and the units and activities we had developed, things like that.

So I told Rose, "You tell me what you do, and I'll type it for you." I sat down at the typewriter, and she began to tell me. I was at that typewriter for about three hours straight, and my back was really hurting me. I was sitting trying to brace my back because of my missing ribs. Across from us was an open door to another classroom, and because there was nobody in there, the lights were off. So I was sitting there with Rose, and I said, "I'm going to get up and walk around a little bit, and then I'll come back. Before I stood, I happened to look at that door, and Wally Knight was standing there smiling, and he was pointing at me.

I said, "Yahhh!" and I looked away and then looked up again; and he just went out of sight into that room. Rose looked at me, and I said, "Rose, I just saw a ghost!"

She said, "Where?"

"Over there in the doorway. I saw Wally Knight's ghost!"

I got up, and I went over there to that doorway, and I said in Indian, "Whoever you are, or whatever you are trying to do, you just get away!" I said that as I walked around that empty room and then came out.

Eventually, I sat back down at the typewriter again and started to work on Rose's report. I had typed for a couple more hours, and gee, my back was really hurting me. So I told her, "We've got most of it done, so you should try to write the rest down and finish it on your own. I'm going to rest a bit; my back is hurting so bad I can't stand it."

I was just about to stand. I looked toward that door, and there was Wally Knight standing there, smiling just like he did in life. He was pointing and motioning for me to come talk to him! I didn't dare say anything this time, so I just put my head down on the desk and rested a minute. When I looked up, he was gone; so I stood up and called to Chris, "Let's go out and get something to drink. I'm really tired, and my back is killing me."

"Oh, okay," she said. And here, Eugene Henderson, the bus driver, came into the room, and he said, "Madonna, what's the matter with you?

"Nothing." I answered.

"No, I think you should see a doctor; you're as white as a sheet."

"No, there's nothing wrong with me." I said.

"No, I think you should see a doctor, and I'm going to take you right now!"

Chris said, "Come on. I'll go with you."

So we all went out and got in Eugene's car and drove up to the hospital. I got out of the car and walked in. I opened the door, the warm air hit me, and that's the last I remember. Next thing I knew, I was in the hospital, and a nurse named Mary Bowman was standing over me. She said, "Madonna, they're going to fly you out to Bismarck."

"Fly me out? For what?" I asked her.

"Doctor thinks you should go over there," she said quietly.

"But I don't want to go anywhere. Christmas time is the most fun time of the year to be with the kids. I don't want to go any place. Just let me stay here, I should be well enough." I pleaded with her.

She just shook her head and said, "No, you can't, Madonna. It's the doctor's orders."

Soon Dr. Borouski came in and said, "Madonna we're going to fly you to Bismarck, and Sister Depazzie is going to ride along and keep you company." So they did. They took us that afternoon to Ellsworth Air Force Base in an ambulance. From there they flew us to Bismarck, North Dakota.

I was in Bismarck [in] December, January, February, and March. I'd had a slight stroke. I was kind of paralyzed on the left side. So I guess Wally Knight had come to take me with him, but I didn't go. He was a good man, and I think he wanted me to be in a good place.[17] I recovered, but I was never strong enough to go back to the classroom. I carried an oxygen bottle all the time now. After that I worked on and off as a Head Start home-school coordinator but I missed my classroom and my kids.

 Levi Comes for Me

THEY TOOK ME to the hospital in Bismarck, North Dakota. I had a stroke and had pneumonia in my remaining lung, and I was very sick. They flew me in an air ambulance. I remember when they put me on the plane, and Mom said crying, "Mi Cinksi, please get well, mi cinksi." The next thing I remember, I was in the hospital. I kept losing consciousness.

During one of those times I lost consciousness, Levi In The Woods appeared to me. He was calling to me to go with him. Suddenly I saw a long log hall, so I came into the door. I was following Mom and Cousin Mary. I stood there looking for Mom or somebody I might know. I was looking around, and I saw them sitting in the northwest corner of the hall. Every person in the gathering was dead except Mom, Aunt Matilda, and Cousin Mary. They made room for me, and I sat down.

I kept looking around; some of the people I didn't know. The ones I recognized were all deceased! My relatives! It was a gathering, a dance, and they were all in their Indian clothes. There was my Cousin Marceline, and my Aunt Mary High Pine, and my Aunt Emma, Mary's first cousin, and my Grandma Julia High Pine! There was also some of my Lone Eagle relations, grandmas (great aunts) on my grandmother's side; they were all there! I had a grandma named Medicine Boy, she was there, and her daughter. "They are all dead and gone," I thought.

So there I sat watching; there was a man up front making announcements. He said, "Naslo hon wacipelo wayun ciptelo (Everybody round dance)." Singers started hitting the drum and singing. Everybody got up and started making a circle. My Grandma High Pine didn't get up, because she was lame, but she sat there smiling and tapping her toes to the music.

I was sitting there wondering at all of this, when Cousin Mary said, "Let's join in." And here, my mom put a shawl over me and Mary. Even Aunt Matilda Chasing Hawk joined in; she was dancing, too. So we were dancing along, and here, this man came up behind me and said, "Somebody wants to see you out there," pointing to the back of the hall. So I asked him who it was. "I don't know," he said, "but there is a man out there, and he says he must see you right away."

I left the circle and started walking towards the door. I got to the door, opened it, and here it was Levi! And Gee! The hills were green, and covered with flowers all over the ground! There was every kind of tree, and it was so pretty there. Prettier than any place I had ever been. There were birds of every kind, and they were singing. The colors were so beautiful! Levi In The Woods was standing a short ways from me, and he said, "Come here. I want to tell you something." So I started walking towards him, and as I approached him he would move back away from me; but I kept following him.

Finally, I stopped and asked, "What do you want?"

He said, "Come with me over here, I want to tell you something." So I walked towards him; as I did, he kept moving away from me. So I just followed him.

Levi was down the path from me, and that path was such a beautiful place. There was every kind of tree you can think of and flowers along the edge of the path. So I'd stop and smell the flowers. The birds were singing; it was such a pretty sound they were making. I was just taking my time listening and smelling the flowers as I went.

Levi would stop and smile when I would stop. Pretty soon Levi would call me, and I'd follow again. We had gotten quite a way from the dance hall, and I thought, "If Levi chases me, I can't run very fast, so I shouldn't get too far from the people in the hall." So I just stopped, and I said, "You come up here and tell me. I can't go anymore."

"No! You come over here," he pleaded. "I'm not going to take long."

So I started in again—I followed him. He went down a long hill. When he reached the bottom of the hill, I said, "I can't walk up hills very good, so I'm staying here. You tell me from there."

"Please," he said, "You come down here. It's important!" There was a stream down below the hill. It was a beautiful blue color, and it was so clear you could see every rock on the bottom. It was not like any stream I had ever seen at home.

I stood on the little hilltop looking down at the blue stream and said, "I can't come down. You tell me from there."

"No. Come on down here!" he insisted.

"Well," I thought, "If it's that important to him, I'll go down there." When I got down there, I thought to myself, "You know, this man is dead, and I'm talking to him. Now he's trying to get me through that water. I'd better not go through that water, or I'll die." So I just stood there, and Levi started through the water. He was up to his knees in water, then his waist.

"Come and wade in the water with me; it's not cold," he said. "It's really warm. These rocks won't hurt your feet."

"But," I said, "Oh! I can't wade in the water with my bare feet. I'm just going to leave my shoes on."

I started into the water, and it was warm and so clear! He kept moving away from me across the stream, smiling at me. I just kept going, and soon the water was up to my knees. But he just kept going. Soon the water was up to his chest. So I said, "I'm not going any further—this is as far as I'm going!"

I thought, "Well, I'm going to turn around and go back." So I did—I turned around and started coming back. "Come here," he asked again. "I'm going to tell you something important."

"No! I'm going to go back!" I told him. I reached the water's edge and started up the hill.

I stopped half way, to rest, but he was following, so I just kept going. I was so short of breath, but I just kept going, walking towards that beautiful path. Still he was following! Now I was breathing so hard it hurt my chest. "If I make it back to that log hall, I'll be all right," I thought. I just kept walking, and here, somebody slapped my face, calling to me, "Donna? Donna? What's the matter? What's the matter, Donna?" the nurse was saying. I was just sweating! She asked, "Did you have a dream?"

"Yea," I finally said. "I guess it was a dream."

"Where did you go? Who did you go with?" she asked. "You were really talking when you came out of it. We thought we had lost you," the nurse said, smiling.

"I was with Levi," I tried to explain. "I think he wanted

to take me! And I think I was in the place where all my dead relatives are. That must be wherever I was." Saying this before I was awake enough to realize trying to tell this to the nurse wasn't making any sense.

It was such a different experience. It was so vivid. I remember Grandma High Pine so distinctly, sitting there tapping her toe to the drum beat. She always wore a maza wapeyaka [concho belt]. She wore kind of a dark blue dress and a single strand necklace. And my Cousin Marceline, when she was living, always wore a long cotton dress and a wide leather belt. She had that belt on, and she had a blue scarf on her hair. I think she was buried in that. It was so real.

I have never had a dream like that! I believe I must have been close to death. It is a beautiful, wonderful place there. Since that time I haven't been afraid of death. I know what's on the other side. It's a beautiful place, and Levi wants me to join him there.[18]

 College: 1974

I HAD A CHANCE to go to the University of South Dakota in 1974. I was feeling strong that summer, and I wanted to finish my degree. From the times I had gone to college or taken classes through Head Start, I had accumulated one hundred thirty hours of college work. There was even a time in 1973 and 1974 when I had taught Lakota language for the Cheyenne River Community College; but my credits were not organized in a major, so I still had to take classes. I enrolled in the fall and was excited about going to a university. The oxygen bottles I carried to class were small, but still I was able to make most of my classes.

I had a roommate assigned to me; maybe they picked her for me because we were both "Indians." Her name was Pramela Rath, and she was from India. She was kind of a strange one, and even though she was darker skinned than me, she explained that she was from a wealthy family in India, from a good group or whatever. She told me that she did not like having me for a roommate, and that she would see if she could change it.

I said, "That's all right with me, if you are not happy here with me." I think maybe my oxygen bottle scared her, or she thought I still had TB.

There were and are a lot of people who think they can catch disease from those that had TB. I've had that experience often, and I suppose it's the main reason I'm telling all this. Often people won't drink out of clean glasses at my house or drink from a cup I give them. My sister-in-law won't let the grandchildren over to my house. That's one of the things I feared most back in the san, that I will always have to go through life like a leper.[19] Well, anyway, that's the way Pramela treated me.

She didn't have to put up with me for very long, because towards the end of fall semester the winter, the class load and the trouble between me and Pramela took their toll. I got sicker and sicker, until I had to leave school. I ended up in the hospital in Yankton. After a while the doctors said I was well enough to go home, but I was not well enough to try college.

Austin's Trouble

WHEN AUSTIN WAS growing up, he usually made us very proud. He did well in sports and in his courses, and so he began to talk about college. "Auntie Donna, I'm thinking of going to college when I finish high school. I'm thinking of going to Arizona State!"

"Arizona State sounds like a fine school!" I told him. But so far, I couldn't help think.

One time in his senior year he got into trouble. His folks were having trouble with him, and I felt a change in him; so did Jay. The next thing I heard, he was in trouble with some other boys. One was from Cherry Creek, the other from Eagle Butte. They had taken someone's car and broken in somewhere! The police were supposed to be looking for him. I was very frightened for him.

The next night it was very late when I heard someone at the window. I recognized Austin's voice. "Come in, Austin," I whispered, not turning on the light. Austin came in, and he looked just awful.

"Auntie Donna, I'm in trouble, and the police are looking for me. I didn't mean to scare you, but I didn't know what else to do! I'm scared of what the police might do, that I'll go to the Penitentiary."

Austin was looking at the floor. "I know all about it, son. I don't think it is as bad as you think it is. They know boys do things sometimes, but you are making it real bad on yourself running from it. This thing is like a storm, and it will pass.

"Remember the story I told you from Grandma, how back then a storm was coming. A man rode by the house and said, 'A tornado is coming, and it's coming right this way! You better leave—it's already killed animals and destroyed houses!' 'No, I'll stay here!' Unci said.

"So then she went into the house and got her little pipe. When she was ready, she came outside. By then the storm was close, the wind was blowing things around, and the dust made the air brown.

"Grandma just pointed her pipe stem at that storm and she prayed, 'Grandfathers above and in the four directions, please hear me. Grandfathers above, spare this house, I'm praying! Grandfathers!' She prayed, and that storm split and went on either side, close by the house, but she was safe."

When I was finished, I looked over at Austin, it seemed as if his mind had settled down a little. "So you see, son, you have to face this thing; you can't run from it."

"Well, then, what should I do?" he asked, tears in his eyes.

"Go to the police tell them what happened. Tell them

the truth, if it was your idea or not, and if you were in on it. Then take what comes to you. Don't let it ruin what you've done in life so far. Maybe those other boys don't have plans or dreams, but you do."

Austin went to the tribal police, and it worked out for him so that he could continue with things. Austin was not a saint, but he was growing into a fine young man, and I was proud.[20]

                              Don't Give Up!

WHEN AUSTIN FIRST spoke of college, he had wanted to go to Arizona State or a college in California. I can't remember the name of the college. When he was a junior, he went to see the BIA education officer at Eagle Butte.

They told us Austin could not go to college out of state. "We don't do that anymore, give out-of-state education grants. The tuition at those schools is too high. We just don't do that anymore," was all the officer kept saying. But I know others received grants to go out of state. I think because Austin was denied chances to do things like go to an out-of-state school, he began to feel sort of down. He said one day, "I don't know if going to college in South Dakota would do me any good. I don't even know if college would do me any good, because I'm an Indian."

I told him about my Grandpa Puts and of the things he told me about white people. I told him about 1951 and Dr. Meyers. I told him about all the years I had hated white people, and how Sanitor had changed my feelings about all of that.

I also told him, "Even if we feel as if the whole world is white people, and they are all against us, there is still hope! We are Lakota, and we should never give up! We should keep going! There are people that have it much worse than we do. Just little things, little obstacles, should not put in our mind the idea to give up." I told him, "If you give

up now, it will be that way—you'll always be doing that for
the rest of your life!"

Grandma Lucy used to really talk to him. I think because he respects our mom so much, he'd listen to what
she had to say. He respected me, too, and he respected
what we wanted for him. We told him we would try to help
if he decided to go to college and if he did what was necessary to succeed in school. Austin usually did the right
thing by us; he never did sass back. He'd always at least
listen to us; then he'd think about it.

Later that summer Austin came to me and said, "I've
been thinking about all the things you said, and I've decided to go on to school." So he did! He enrolled at South
Dakota State College in Brookings as a business major.

We tried to send him a little money at least once a
month, sometimes more often. I'd save money from the
rent, and [send] some of the money I'd saved from grocer-
ies and the phone bill. If I was really careful, I'd have thirty
dollars a month to send him. Mom and I would combine
whatever we could and send that to him.

You know all boys like to eat. We didn't want him to go
hungry. That was why we sent him money. We told him,
"We'll send you money as long as you don't use it for drugs
or to get drunk," things like that. I suppose he was like
every other human being—he probably tried all those
things, but he never made it a habit!

                                      Austin's College Years

THERE WAS A TIME when Austin told us he'd quit school!
He said, "I'm tired of going to school. I don't think it will
do me any good to finish college, because even if I do, I
won't be able to get a job, especially here on the reservation!" He seemed real serious this time.

It seemed like while he was in college there were always
financial difficulties: late checks from the BIA, or waiting

for grant money to reach the college. I think that each year it must have been harder for him to go back and register or find a place to stay with almost no money at all.

That summer I called the BIA education office at the Aberdeen area office. They said, "Just go ahead and tell him to go to school. We'll send the money directly to the college."

Then we really talked to Austin, "You can have a good future, don't feel down about your chances. College will be a big help to you in your life, in ways you can't see now. You should finish."

He thought about it for a long while and then coming quietly to us said, "I've thought about it a long time, what you've both said. I'll go back and try to finish." I was very happy for him.

                              Victory Trill

THE DAY CAME; Austin's graduation from college was drawing near. I had promised Austin and myself many times that if Austin graduated from the University, I would live long enough to see it. Now I had kept my promise, and I was happy.

Austin means a lot to me! I think that if it were not for him I would have given up many times. Even now, when I have really bad days with my breathing, I stop and I think about him. Not only about him—I have others that I love very much. I think about all of them, and I get up, and I brace up, and I go! Austin gave me so much courage. He is a pride and joy in my life.

Mom was very excited about Austin's accomplishment, and she was teaching me to make the trill sound Lakota women make when they are proud, when their men have made them proud.[21] "Le le le le le! Le le le le le!" I practiced moving my tongue that way, practiced the trill for his graduation day.

My mother, Jay, Carol Swan, and I went to the graduation in Brookings in one car, Sidney and Shirley Keith,
Jerry and the Hertels (Austin's oldest sister) and their
family in another car.

I was happy driving towards South Dakota State University, going over in the car. We were all happy and excited this day.

December 17, 1979, Austin Paul's graduation, was the
happiest day of my life! This was the realization of a dream
I had for him since he was a little boy. We had hoped and
prayed for him all those years, that one day he would
graduate from college. And Mom lived to see it! No one in
our family had ever finished college, and I wanted him to
be the first. So it was really a very happy occasion for all
of us.

I was relieved that it was, for me, all over. I thought
over all the obstacles he had encountered in school. I remembered the problems we had all had to overcome to
help Austin to this wonderful day. All these thoughts en-
tered my mind, of the dreams I had kept of finishing college, thoughts of the years, the good times, the hard times,
my bad health, all these filled me as I sat in the auditorium,
waiting impatiently for his name to be read aloud.

I had told Austin, "If I live to that day, the day you graduate, I'm going to be there and I'm going to make the sound,
because I will be so happy, so proud you have graduated."
They called his name, Austin Paul Keith. Austin walked up
onto the platform. Grandma and I stood and we made the
sound, the Sound of Praise. "Le le le le le le le!"

EIGHT YEARS have passed since most of the stories in this collection were recorded. These years have brought many changes to the lives of the people close to Madonna.

Austin has married and is a dad working for the tribal college in Eagle Butte. He remains, as ever, very close to Madonna. Shirley and Sidney have moved to Rapid City but play an active role both there and home at Cheyenne River. They are now grandparents and even great-grandparents.

Manuel, Madonna's oldest brother, suffered a cerebral hemorrhage in the summer of 1980. His death had a profound effect on Madonna and their mother, Lucy Swan. It was as if his passing stole her taste for life.

Until that time Lucy had been a very fit octogenarian with a tremendous youthfulness and humor. As late as that year she still attended powwows and sang honoring songs at the wakes and funerals of veterans. She spoke on the need for commodity foods in communities with no stores; she spoke of the needs of the young and to them about how they should live their lives—and all of it with obvious love. Grandma Lucy, as she was lovingly called by all who knew her, was still continuously sought as an expert on many aspects of Lakota Sioux culture. She shared her knowledge of some areas in art and music that were all but lost.

With the passing of her firstborn, Lucy's buoyant health and outlook began to change. Not long after Manuel's death Grandma began to speak of going home. "Home" to her was the place where Jesus, her boys, and her husband had gone. The years alone had put her late husband's memory in a very different perspective. She had resolved her hurt and longed to be with "the only man I ever loved."

Lucy saw her own death as a joyous occasion, a release

from this earthly plane. Toward the end we tried to spend
time with her. She called to me one day. Her voice was
weak, but she had a grin on her tired face. "Takoja, I want
you to do something for me. All these people who are
coming around crying, sad that I am dying, please try to
keep them away from me. Tell them to stay away from me.
I'm not sad! I'm happy! I'm going home, home to see my
boys, home to see James, home to see Jesus!"

"So!" she said with a soft chuckle. "I don't want to see
sad people around me."

During her last days Lucy would move easily from this
world to the spirit world and back, seeing and conversing
with her loved ones in that other land. Her faith, strong to
the moment she left this earth, was a singular blend of traditional Lakota beliefs and world view with fundamentalist
Catholicism. Grandma Lucy's death, one of true joy and
expectation, is something that will stay with me as long as
I live.

Erskin, the youngest brother, still resides in that house.

With the passing of Lucy, I almost expected, consider-
ing the frail nature of her health, that Madonna would join
her mother. Their relationship was deep and close, and
the loss rocked Madonna to her very foundation. But I
misread her, as had all the doctors and nurses.

At least two factors seemed to provide her with the will
to go on. First is the Lakota attitude toward death, which
is, briefly, that death constantly surrounds the living and is
a natural part of life and that the living must go on. Suffering is a natural part of human existence; self-pity is a
luxury reserved for others.

The second reason may be more easy to understand.
With the passing of her mother, Madonna became the matriarch of her family, assuming the role of ritual leader, the
arbiter of spats and disputes, the unifying personality in
her extended family. Her sense of obligation to her many
nephews and nieces, to her community and tribe, pushed
her onward.

Small wonder, then, that Madonna's role actually

Madonna being congratulated as Native American Woman of the Year by Ken West, tribal vice chairman, Cheyenne River Reservation, 1983.

broadened. Continuing to live in Cherry Creek, she served on the board of the Tri-Community Development Co-operative and as a member of the tribal hiring, firing, and grievance committee. One would have to live in a tribal setting to fully appreciated the delicate nature of this position.

In 1983, Madonna was selected as the North American Indian Woman of the Year by her tribal sisters at Cheyenne River. Still she claimed she didn't know what the fuss was about!

I have visited with Madonna only infrequently since then, but when I see her I am convinced anew of her durability as a respected elder.

Although she is increasingly confined to the house and her oxygen-generating machine, her conversation is generally of others and their problems or triumphs.

Her one complaint is that people don't visit her as often as they used to; but I take this with a grain of salt, because

people still honor her as matriarch and visit her daily, seeking advice, comfort, and company. When I visited her in
the summer of 1987, no fewer than six people from her
community stopped by to "check on her"!

More often these days she talks, as her mother once
did, of "going home." I cannot predict, nor have the doctors, how much longer we will be blessed with her on this
earth.

Madonna took a great personal risk to relate these
stories. It is her fondest hope that they will inspire others,
particularly the young. I know that as long as I live her
memory and the pure wisdom of her stories will be with
me daily.

MARK ST. PIERRE

Steamboat Springs, Colorado

Notes

Part One

1. This "giveaway" remains a standard social ritual (with spiritual overtones) among the Lakota. It is likely that Lucy vowed to conduct a giveaway if Manuel survived the first year. This giveaway was in wopila, or thanksgiving.

2. The items Madonna mentions (I had also heard this story from Lucy) would have been standard items of the day for an upper-class Lakota family. The more "important" the event, in this case the birth of Manuel who was chaske', or first born, the more prestigious were the gifts. The status of first-born male is of critical importance to the Lakota because this person will carry on culturally based family rituals in the future. The training of this child may be quite different from that of succeeding children. It is unlikely that such giveaways were held for succeeding children.

Madonna received the status of winona, or first-born female, and thus also received additional ritual training and attention, that she might keep these things alive and know how to conduct female rituals.

Lucy risked arrest by staging a giveaway for Manuel because giveaways violated several orders from the Indian Service. The Bureau of Indian Affairs felt the dispersement of wealth in this traditional manner slowed the progress of the Sioux toward civilization.

3. The infant mortality rate during this period was extremely high. Characteristically, Madonna downplayed bad things that happened; she always was genuinely thankful for what her family had. I never once heard Lucy express self-pity in regard to her children's early deaths, both because such deaths were not unusual and because it is part of the cultural ideal for Lakota women not to complain about their problems.

4. Chilooco is an old Indian school still operating in Oregon. Its curriculum during James's years would have been similar to a trade school oriented toward agriculture.

That James went on to school is unusual. He received the equivalent to a junior-college education at Haskell, likely emphasizing bookkeeping and secretarial skills. Haskell still survives as Haskell Indian College. Although it is governed by an all-Indian board, the school still is heavily influenced by the BIA.

5. "Chiefs' houses" were given as fulfillment of treaty agreements and also as "acknowledgments" to significant headmen

who encouraged their people toward civilization. These houses
were tiny Victorian structures brought up the river and then
freighted by wagon and erected on the land of the chief. These
certainly would have been the most formal houses of the day in
Indian country. Only one of these houses still survives in South
Dakota; it sits on its original site in White Horse community on
the Cheyenne River Reservation.

6. This comment refers to a specific set of concepts exempli-
fied by those who were born and lived during the nomadic days
before the Custer battle and the subsequent final confinement.
These people were thought to exemplify the cultural values and
practices which form the modern ideas about what is or was
traditional.

The term Sioux is misleading since it has no specific reference
within Lakota people's history. They call themselves Sioux when
giving their tribal name to non-Indians, but within the tribe call
themselves Lakota, which means "The Allies." Sioux is said to be
a shortening of the Ojibwa word Naddowissi (Lesser Snakes,
Adders, or enemy) with a French plural ending ioux, thus becoming Naddowissioux, which was shortened over time to Sioux.

In a real sense the term Sioux refers to all tribes of the loose
confederation known as the Oceti Sakowin or Seven Council
Fires. Within this confederation (which may have been more
philosophical than practical) were three main divisions. The Dakota (Eastern Division) comprised four "seats" and were made
up of the Midé Wakanton (Spirit Lake people), the Wakpé Kuté
(Shooters Amongst the Leaves), the Sissitoin (Fish Scale Dwellers), and Whapeton (Leaf Dwellers). These Dakota people live
today on various reservations in South Dakota, North Dakota,
Minnesota, Montana, and Canada.

The Nakota (Middle) were comprised of the two Ihanktowan
or Yankton (End Dwellers) groups which occupied two "seats" on
the mythical Council. The final group, and the group from
which Madonna's ancestry sprung, are the Lakota (Western).

Although in earlier times the Lakota comprised only one "seat"
in the Seven Council Fires, they eventually grew in strength and
numbers. By 1775 they had crossed the Missouri River and had
become subdivided into Seven Tribes themselves. Within that
time frame they acquired the horse and became the buffalo-
hunting warriors of legend.

The bands or tribes are from largest to smallest as follows: the
Oglala on the Pine River Reservation, South Dakota; the Sićaŋǵu
(Brulé) on Rosebud and Lower Brulé Reservations in South Da-
kota; the Minneconjou (Plants by the Water People, of which Chief

White Swan, Madonna's paternal grandfather was a significant
warrior and Head Man), who live in the large villages of Cherry
Creek, Red Scaffold, and Bridger on the southern half of the
Cheyenne River Reservation; the Hunkpapa (Camps at the
Horn, Sitting Bull's People), who live in the South Dakota por-
tion of the Standing Rock Reservation near McLaughlin, South
Dakota; the Itazipco (Sans Arc or Bowless Band), who are the
traditional keepers of the Sacred Calf Pipe and live along the
Moreau River on the Cheyenne River Reservation; the two small-
est groups, largely intermarried today, the O-ohé Nunpa (Two
Kettle) on the east end of Cheyenne River and the Si Sapa or
Blackfeet Sioux living in the Northeastern part of Cheyenne
River Reservation and on Standing Rock. The Lakota comprise
by far the largest "Sioux" population today, numbering some
seventy thousand.

Each of the three major subdivisions is characterized by differences in dialect and, to some extent, differences in their cultural
orientation. The Dakota were Woodlands or Park Lands people
with ties to other Woodlands tribes, sharing some of their cos-
mology and world view; the Yankton occupied a vast territory
east of the Missouri River and shared traits with other river
peoples such as agriculture and occasionally earth lodges (Drift-
ing Goose's Band); the Lakota shared in common with other
High Plains peoples a unique religious and philosophical system,
including the Sun Dance and Vision Quest.

7. To pray with the pipe is a shortened way of expressing the
idea that he lived the old pre-Christian religion and may imply
that he did not participate in any Christian denomination.

In a literal sense it refers to a short but formal personal ritual
consisting of the "loading" of a pipe and simultaneous singing of
a pipe-filling song, the singing of a set of songs to the four directions or to a specific spirit helper, and the ritual smoking of the
tobacco that has been offered up. Almost every Lakota ritual has
this ritual within it. It is said that in the old days men and women
got up with the morning star to pray with the pipe, thanking the
Grandfathers for blessings and praying for help and guidance in
the coming day.

8. The sweat bath, or oinikage (to make a sweat), is the Lakota's central purification ritual and precedes any major ritual or
curing ceremony. The lodge is constructed of willows which are
bent and driven into the earth and then covered with buffalo
robes, or today with quilts and tarpulins. The specific rituals performed in the sweat bath depend on the purpose of the purification. The ceremony is conducted in the darkened lodge with

temperatures reaching 160 degrees. The heat comes from red-
hot rocks previously heated in a ritual bier. See William Powers,
Oglala Religion (Lincoln: University of Nebraska Press, 1977).

9. Wild turnips are actually a tuber root (*Psoralea lanceolata*)
not at all related to the turnip. These roots were peeled, reveal-
ing a white interior, dried, and then (by means of the cleaned
root stem) braided into long strings for storage. These timpsila,
a staple of the Lakota diet, still are gathered and used for special
occasions. As "wild turnips" usually ripen in July, this reference
also sets the relative time of the story.

10. The indication would be that they were praying for the
health of one of the men. James Aplan, a regionally recognized
authority on the Lakota, grew up in Fort Pierre, South Dakota,
where his parents operated a trading post. He says he doubts
sweat lodges were a part of Sioux life during the 1930s; nonethe-
less, oral accounts of the sweat bath have come to me from numerous elderly Lakota.

11. Ceremonies involving the direct intercession of or use of a
spirit helper follow a strict, if individualized, ritual. The virgin—
still employed in some contemporary ceremonies, such as the
sun dance—represents a purity that, it is thought, appeals to
the spirits in question and thereby helps the supplicant contact
the supernatural.

12. "The Grandfathers" is a generic term used to describe the
spirits of sacred animals or ancestors who might aid in the making of a medicine object such as a bundle, shield, or rattle. These
creatures might also grant sacred insight for a cure or in finding
a lost object or sacred enlightenment.

13. This tipi had significance for a number of reasons. First, it
was a buffalo-hide tipi that had survived in family hands since
the 1870s. Second, it was painted with personal helper spirit im-
ages. Third, it had the markings indicating White Swan had been
a headman. It may also be that a personal vow had been made by
Puts On His Shoes to erect the tipi each summer as a memorial
to his beloved brother.

14. It was not uncommon for the elderly to live and receive
guests in a tent, nor is it uncommon even today for Sioux people
to move into a wall tent during the hot prairie summer when the
interior of a frame house may not cool until midnight.

15. The sun dance, as a procreative rite, is used in the suppli-
cation to Wakon Tonka, (God, the Great Mystery, personified by
the sun) for new life across the spectrum of creation—plant, animal, and human. Using the sun dance for the breaking of a
drought would be consistent with Lakota religious theory.

16. This is an unusual attitude for a Lakota and may have

been a personal aesthetic or a product of his off-reservation schooling. James does, however, opt to participate in ·a buffalo hunt two years later.

17. This story tells much about the traditional values of the Lakota. Puts On His Shoes displays the value of "long suffering" in the quiet way in which he handles his sorrow; then he displays "generosity" in the old sense, giving expensive things not tied to reciprocity, such as his tipi, wagon, and horses.

18. From the language used to tell this story it would seem, again, that the tipi was erected each summer as a personal vow to the memory of White Swan. This is not usual; it could be that the tipi had a spiritual significance or it could merely represent the fact that this was a proud and unusual family.

19. Red Scaffold is a community of approximately four hundred Howodsju (Minneconjou) Lakota located in the south central part of Cheyenne River Reservation. It is considered to be a "full-blood" community.

20. Cherry Creek had an ancestral tie for James. The oldest village on Cheyenne River, it also is the largest, with a current population approximating one thousand. Consisting of various sub-bands of the Minneconjou, the village generally is considered a full-blood community.

21. In nonindustrial nonurban cultures, the traditional divisions of labor between males and females persist both in fact and in the folklore and thinking of the people.

Madonna's comment on how there was more time for the enjoyment of life when "there were more women to share the work" speaks to the reality of this division in a hunting-gathering culture even as it underwent drastic change in the early twentieth century. This division of labor and the sharing of work tasks by sex group led both to the establishment of "bands" early in human evolution and to the practice of plural marriage and recognition of extended family. Put simply, attitudes and beliefs change much more slowly than technology

22. I first heard this story from Lucy Swan. Madonna's version follows her mother's very closely.

23. Rectangular wall tents quickly replaced the tipi as the common shelter for the summer. Usually pitched beside tiny log houses in which the family spent the winter, wall tents required short poles that were reusable and locally available. This was advantageous, as the prairie reservation offered no tall pines for people to cut for tipi poles. The wall tent was also a part of annuities and was easily made or purchased ready-made from the reservation traders. These tents remain the common Lakota summer shelter.

24. Bravery was a central cultural value for Lakota women. This story is almost allegorical to the traditional concept of female bravery.

25. White River, a sub-agency for annuities, became a "white" town during the homestead period (1910–1915). A number of Sićanǵu Lakota communities still are adjacent to the town.

26. The "farm agent" may have been a very early version of a county agent; however, he may actually have been a boss farmer employed by the BIA to teach the Indians agricultural and ranching skills.

27. Self-effacement, a central feature of Lakota humor, is a culturally acceptable means of bringing attention to oneself.

28. Scotty Phillips was married to a Cheyenne River woman and was known by, and sympathetic to, the Sioux people. Many credit him with preserving the American bison in South Dakota. His contribution has grown into the prolific herd now residing in Custer State Park.

29. In reviewing the manuscript, Madonna commented that she did not like her version of the story, saying it lacked significant details. We did not come up with a better version, so hers stands.

30. Hu blaska translates as "false" or "ghost" turnip. It closely resembles the standard wild turnip, or timpsila, but it has a long, thick root and is not edible.

31. Apparently, these sleds of buffalo ribs lashed with rawhide were common winter toys used by Lakota children, who spent most of the day outside the tipi.

32. Inyan Hoksila, Stone Boy or Rock Boy, was half-supernatural and half-human; thus, he had many characteristics of both. According to the late Joe Rockboy, a Yankton Sioux elder, one of Inyan Hoksila's magical qualities was his extreme "density" or weight.

33. It would certainly seem consistent with Lucy's attitudes that she would allow her children to play with white children. She seemed to have a love for all humanity. It was not common for those whites growing up on near a reservation to have some friends who were Indian.

34. As stated earlier, the BIA taught agricultural skills both on the reservation and in the boarding schools.

35. This passage again indicates that Madonna felt they had more than enough material possessions and were more fortunate than most of her neighbors.

36. During the early part of John Collier's appointment as Commissioner of Indian Affairs under Franklin Roosevelt, "day schools" were established in reservation communities to lessen

the severe emotional and cultural confusion brought on by sending very young children to boarding schools. This reference is to
one such school in Cherry Creek.

37. Lucy Swan, a devout Catholic, sent Madonna to Stephan
Mission for her schooling. It seems that, although loneliness was
always a problem, Madonna liked the school and most of the Sisters who worked there. The school is still functioning on the edge
of the Crow Creek Indian Reservation.

38. The cause of these fainting spells is uncertain. The fact
that Lucy referred to these seizures as "when I would die," because she had no memory of dreams when she was unconscious,
lends significant insight into Lakota worldview.

39. It is unfortunate that this passage of a female performing
a shamanic rite is rare in literature about Plains Indians. It is,
however, not a particularly rare occurrence, according to many
surviving oral accounts of holy women in family histories. It is
further insightful that the Catholic priests on the reservation had
warned the Lakota to stay away from these medicine people, and
by 1910, had enough influence to be considered in the decision.

40. This "doctoring" ceremony was held in the daytime. Today
ceremonies such as this are held in the dark. The blowing of various colors from the hand and the bird noises, critical manifesta-
tions of the sacred, are examples of the woman's "power" and
spirit helper. The skeptic might consider them sleight-of-hand.

41. Use of the buffalo horn or "sucking" as a means of remov-
ing a negative or foreign influence from the body is common
among circumpolar groups. Removal of the foreign object from
the patient assured the cure. To the faithful, in the proper cultural setting this "proof" would have had profound psychobio-
logical efficacy. Mrs. Thin Elk also further strengthened her cure
by announcing, "She will never die like that again," putting her
reputation on the line to assure success.

42. Offering expensive gifts in wopila, or thanksgiving, follows standard Lakota procedure and is still the common way of
handling fees for services today. If a family is very poor, the fee
can be as little as a meal and a pack of cigarettes.

43. The forms of coercion used to encourage Lakota parents
to send their children to school included denial of rations and
annuities, which placed families in the position of starving or going along with government policy. Some births were not reported, in order to keep their children at home. It is likely that
this man was an employee of the BIA and was in charge of finding and forcing these children off to school so that they might
grow up "civilized."

44. Lucy's curriculum, a half day of domestic and agricultural

experience and a half day of "academics," was typical of the day. Many older Sioux people lament the passing of this type of school experience, saying that children today "don't learn how to do anything [practical]!"

45. The story of the ruination of her elk-tooth dress was one of Grandma Lucy's favorites. It never failed to produce a great heartfelt chuckle. An elk-tooth dress, certainly an heirloom, was the most prestigious fashion of the nineteenth century because each elk has only two teeth suitable, and a dress may have had as many as 160 teeth.

46. This combination of traditional and Anglo domestic skills, along with her minimal formal education, was in fact quite sufficient. Lucy was also from the "right kind of family" and was a very attractive young woman.

47. This establishing of a marriage agreement with the oldest surviving male of the bride's family follows a traditional Lakota pattern; in fact, this was the most formal part of the marriage procedure before Christian procedures were adopted. "Prairie marriages," made without benefit of license or preacher, are still common among the Lakota, who had no formal marriage ceremony after the traditional giving of gifts by the suitor.

48. It would seem that the families who participated in this hunt were mostly members of the same tiyospaye, or extended family group.

49. Even in her eighties, when she was riding in our car, Lucy would often see a certain type of broken country or the signs of ancient buffalo wallows and comment that his would have been a good place to hunt for buffalo.

50. Lucy's eyes would dance as she recounted how the old men became young again killing in the old way once more. The trill sound made by the women to acknowledge their pleasure and pride in the accomplishments of their men is the "Sound of Praise" referred to in this book. Hohnágicala hotoŋpi is the sound a screech owl makes.

51. The placing of the hand to the face while laughing or smiling was a traditional gesture. Done out of habit and formal respect, it is no longer generally practiced.

52. This use of a story to relate a moral attitude or lesson is the most common setting for these stories, and the anecdotal telling was the original setting in which I first heard most of these stories.

53. Leaving a grandchild in the care of the older woman was not unusual–children were often reared by grandparents—but the implication is one of neglect: the mother was off spending an annuity check and generally being irresponsible. This narra-

tive indicates both a long-standing pattern and recent cultural disintegration.

54. The belief that animals have their own culture, language, intelligence, and soul, is profound among the Lakota and continues to a be a central way in which their worldview differs from a Judeo-Christian explanation of nature.

55. This traditional offering to mice spirits is the standard and appropriate response to their "intercession" in saving Julia Brave Eagle and the baby.

56. This short vignette tells of an herbalist performing a cure. There are two distinct, if overlapping, healing traditions among the Lakota: that of the wicasa wakon (holy man or woman), who effects the cure by calling on the sacred, and that of the pejuta wicasa (herb doctor), who uses the knowledge of plants and the intercession of the bear spirit helper to cure. It is significant here that she emitted the sound of the bear while performing the cure. Mrs. Blue Hair had a son named Robert (now deceased) who also was a traditional healer; hence the name of this story.

57. A number of things are inferred about the place of the healer in Lakota society. First, Madonna indicates he was a wicasa wakon and uses the term holy man, indicating also that he had used isolation and fasting to understand the relationship between the natural and spiritual worlds. He was able to send a part of his soul, the sicun, into the spirit realm and learn through intercessors how to help the infirm.

The fact that she uses the terms "sickness" and "problems" subtly indicates her conviction that some problems are personal, even psychological. The last important inference is about the method of payment: "He had many horses and was well liked." Every time a holy man makes a prognostication, he will in some sense be held liable. Because payment was not strictly prescribed and was often in reward for a remarkable recovery, only a truly gifted man could perform this role in a manner that brought him some level of wealth.

58. Hanbleciya, essentially purification, is isolation from food, water, and the community of humans, in some remote spot. This central ritual remains the principle method employed by Plains Indian men and women to acquire a spirit helper or to learn songs or gain insight that will increase their spiritual insight and, by implication, power.

59. Preparation and instruction for the hanbleciya usually take a full year and might also be considered a four-year commitment to the teacher. Also included in this type of relationship is the expectation that a fast will also be conducted each of the four years. Early spring is generally considered the best time to

"put someone on the hill," but other seasons, including the dead of winter, may be used.

60. The tone in Madonna's voice suggests that being staked physically to the fasting place was not unusual in the early 1870s, when this story took place. It certainly would be unusual today. Although placing a small hardwood skewer under the skin of the chest or back is still practiced in association with the sun dance, its use in the fasting rite has been discontinued. It is commensurate with long-standing Lakota beliefs that self-denial, pain, and suffering can help open portals to the sacred.

61. Despite certain technological adaptation (e.g., the car, refrigerator, bottle-gas stove, Christian burial service), very little in the Lakota attitude and approach to death seems to have changed. The attendance of tremendous numbers of mourners (some having traveled long distances) at all-night wakes, funeral services, and feasts, is still typical.

Eulogies may go on for many hours during the wake. Guests are fed by the close relatives of the deceased, and various ministers or Indian gospel groups may be invited to fill the hours before burial. Honoring the dead, especially those revered in life, by means of protracted memorial dinners and giveaway rites on the first four anniversaries of the death, is still a common practice.

62. While this story is self-explanatory, it does remind the listener of the Lakota belief that each animal has a spirit and a form of intelligence suitable to its kind, often with powers and knowledge surpassing those of humans in certain areas.

63. She refers to the Fort Laramie Treaty of 1868. Brave Eagle Woman would have been about eight years old. This treaty, really the first to establish clear boundaries, created the Great Sioux Reservation.

64. This reference indicates the constant threat of starvation faced by high plains hunter-gatherers.

65. The White River?

66. Dreaming and contacting the sacred when dreaming are strong, if informal, practices among present-day Lakota. Discussions of dreams, their content, and their meaning are fairly common in the Lakota household. Movies and literature have had a good time caricaturing the clairvoyance of Indians.

67. Julia indicates here that to the hunter-gatherer culture of her childhood this loss of property could result in suffering and death. Replacement of everything from garments and homes to essential tools and saddlery created temporary problems that affected the entire community. Grief and physical impoverishment left a hunting band open to attack by the winter environment,

starvation, disease, and enemy tribes—a fact not totally appreciable by her daughter or grandchildren.

68. The balancing humor in this statement, typically Lakota, indicates acceptance of life's uncertainties.

69. This passage describes the self-effacement admired and reinforced among the Lakota. More importantly, however, it reveals the challenge of developing a self-concept universal among adolescents.

70. The role of the spiritually mature man in the Lakota family is as spiritual head. In this capacity each man is a priest, and each man can develop his own spirituality without having to be labeled by the community as a holy man. Many young men fasted for a spirit helper but few made of this quest a vocation.

Within this role as "family" priest, a man or sometimes a woman might be the first line of spiritual healing in an emergency or problem of less importance. James's role here is understandable and occasionally manifest in the conversations of reservation people today.

71. Wife beating, discussed among males at many levels, is a subject both admired and condemned. In Lakota society as a whole it is condemned. As in other societies, such abuse occurs most often among adults exposed to it as children.

The more interesting feature of this passage may be the use of the uncle figure to arbitrate family problems, to give sage counsel, and generally try to preserve the family. This pattern is less common today but still operates in some families.

72. Menstrual period.

73. In the pre-reservation society menstruating women were isolated in a small ribbed structure somewhat like a sweat lodge a short distance from the main lodge. Elders such as Joseph Rockboy and Charles Kills Enemy informed me that this was not to disgrace the woman but to isolate her female powers from male spiritual powers, because contact with even the essence of menstrual flow could cancel or remove success from the bundle or weapon. This, the elders are careful to conclude, indicates a tremendous respect for the sacred mystery surrounding female procreative powers. The enclosure made for Madonna fits the old pattern for this ceremony.

74. The pattern of the things done and discussed in this vignette seems to bear a strong resemblance to stories told to me by elderly women about things seen in yukan' kan' (puberty rites) at the turn of the century. Isna tiċa lowan refers to this first tipi of isolation ceremony.

75. During these days, certain cultural virtues and values are elevated to the sacred to impress them indelibly on the soul and

nature of the young woman. Industry, hospitality, generosity, moral courage, sexual knowledge and understanding, the duties of spouse and mother—all are discussed to prepare the child for joining the world of women.

76. This lucid vignette defies comment and adds to published information on the transference and role of explicit and implicit cultural values of Sioux women.

77. This story is classical anecdotal Lakota humor of the type used to share a remembrance or laugh with family or friend. It further indicates a specific time when rummage was introduced to the Cherry Creek community. Rummage clothing still comes into the reservations and is often the source of light-hearted joking, teasing, and perhaps embarrassment. Obviously also about greed, the anecdote reinforces attitudes of generosity and sharing.

78. Vitiligo is a nonfatal loss of pigment, rare in dark-skinned peoples. The doctor's words, as recalled in the story, probably are a misinterpretation of what he actually said—or a product of family oral history.

79. The proper behavior after a funeral is to feed all those in attendance and then to disperse all the goods of the deceased to those gathered. The implications for a quicker return to mental and spiritual health and an adjustment to grief could be discussed here, but the reality of a house completely stripped of its contents certainly tells of a dramatic turning point.

Precious items might go to people named by the dying individual, or to people outside the family but beloved by the deceased (if the deceased was the head of a household), and down the line to lesser acquaintances, until nothing remains except the bare walls.

A less complete version of this giveaway is practically standard following any Lakota funeral. This would include most of the deceased person's clothing and ceremonial dress, if any, as well as quilts, cloth, dishes, and saddles—and new items purchased at the store. Under direct attack by the federal government for many years, the ritual also may have changed with the tribal economy.

In South Dakota the more complete giveaway ritual is still conducted by a few families who might be defined by the larger Lakota community as more traditional or "full blood." Madonna conducted a complete giveaway following Lucy Swan's burial. The writer was present at this funeral.

80. Quick consumption refers here to the spontaneous hemorrhaging of a tubercular hemoptysis in the lungs. It was a cause of death among many people stricken with tuberculosis of the

lung. It was a constant fear of those exposed to TB, including the children at the Mission.

81. Kennel is a community on the Standing Rock Reservation.

82. The constant references to Catholicism indicate the importance of spiritual participation and the dual nature of contemporary Lakota religious expression. Certainly, the Swan family actively integrated these two systems. Joseph Rockboy used to say, "One way of praying is good; two ways is even better." Almost all modern Lakota are baptized into one denomination or another. It is noteworthy that most Lakota holy men working within the traditional religion are baptized Catholics. I am inclined to think this is because of the mystical orientation of Roman Catholic dogma and ritual.

Within the last twenty years the Catholic and Anglican churches have tried to include some aspects of Lakota ritual in their services. When the Rapid City Diocese ordained Bishop Chapput (a Potawatomi), some aspects of Lakota religious ritual were used. Some Catholic priests, particularly Jesuits, see certain positive social effects from encouraging the old beliefs and rituals.

83. Weight loss and cessation of menstrual periods are both symptomatic of advanced tuberculosis.

84. "Pleurisy pains" or "quick consumption," terms commonly used in that day, both referred to tuberculosis but did not sound so final. "Pleurisy pains" refers to pain originating in the pleura serous membrane that makes up the lungs and the walls of the thoracic cavity.

85. "Cloudy lungs" would probably indicate a very active case of TB:

Tuberculosis refers to any of the infectious diseases of man and other animals due to species of the mycobacterium and marked formations of tubercles and caseous necrosis (reduction to a cottage cheese like substance of former living tissue) in tissue of any organ; in man the lung is the usual portal through which infection reaches the other organs.

Mycobacteria are thin, slightly curved, rod-shaped microorganisms two kinds of which cause tuberculosis and leprosy. Once in the body they cause "tubercular pneumonia, formation of tuberculous granulation tissue, caseous necrosis, calcification, and cavity formation.

The above information on TB is taken from *Stein and Day Medical Encyclopedia* (New York: Stein and Day, 1971), 439–40. These calcified cavities can rupture, causing hemoptysis and sudden death. Other symptoms include weight loss, fatigue, night sweats, purulent sputum, and chest pain.

86. Overcrowding is still considered a key variable in the spread of tuberculosis. It is this writer's opinion that drafty tipis were less of a threat when occupied by a large number of people than were the tiny log houses used during Madonna's childhood. *Mycobacterium bovis*, from cows, usually enters the system through unpasteurized milk. The fear of airborne TB from cows and other farm animals killed in the fire is probably folklore, but the identification of TB with cows is not. *Stein and Day,* 439–40.

87. Madonna feels strongly that she acquired TB from farm animals consumed by the prairie fire, that the disease became airborne and infected her. It is natural for those who have survived TB to deny that it might have been contracted at home. This is the result of the social stigma and deep fears created in response to a disease that really had no cure.

The unfortunate reality is that as an airborne pathogen it was present in the environment almost everywhere Madonna lived. It is possible that the damage done to her lungs by the prairie fire may have had a direct influence on her becoming an active TB victim.

88. The infamous red quarantine tags are still the cause of much emotion amongst those Lakota old enough to remember the epidemic. So great is the continuing level of fear of the stigma that people who have been diagnosed as tuberculous still hide their disease, often at the cost of their lives. The knowledge that this disease is curable has not totally eradicated the disease or the fear it instilled in the Lakota.

89. She refers to the sanitorium operated by the U.S. Public Health Service in Rapid City, South Dakota, for containing and "treating" American Indian tuberculosis patients.

Part Two

1. The cultural reality of and functional importance of the traditional extended family is made clear in this passage. While Mrs. Bridwell was not the girl's actual grandmother, Madonna somehow naturally understood and accepted her when she stepped in to play that role. Developed through ritual and daily life, these ties are central to Lakota culture. The resulting social and family relationships often baffle non-Indians concerned with "reservation progress."

2. During this period, ownership of a car by a Lakota was still unusual. Most people still did their regular travel by horse-drawn wagon.

3. The mention of earphones is significant. First, because they kept patients in touch with the outside world, they were the

source of much time-consuming pleasure. Second, Madonna developed a little business repairing headphones for the other patients, a skill she taught herself. She did this for spending money and traded her repairs for things from the other patients

4. It seems that, from her earliest years, Madonna dreamed fervently of a formal education beyond high school. This is interesting, given the fact that Indian schools had only recently encouraged girls to complete high school. Her dream may have been influenced by the fact that her mother enjoyed reading and always wished she had received more education and the fact that her father was very well educated for his day.

5. This common Lakota "superstition" about death is still believed by many.

6. "Death Row" was a grim-humored description for the isolation ward occupied by terminal patients.

7. The community store, in a village large enough to have one, was a social center. Often highly respected, storekeepers provided services beyond selling supplies, such as first aid, "banking," barbering, and access to a phone.

8. Dr. Sedlechek is well remembered by the patients of the Sioux Sanitorium. Madonna describes him as a (WWII) displaced person with a thick accent. Although he is remembered by patients as being mean and tyrannical, this behavior must be contextualized. It is important to consider that the san was probably one of the few places a foreigner could practice medicine and that (at least in the early part of Madonna's stay) he was faced more with containing than with "curing" the disease. In addition, even though he knew there was no cure, every day he risked contracting the disease. Public stigma also extended to those who worked in the san. According to comments made by Gloria Traversy, as late as 1974 many employees lived in housing on the hospital grounds and seldom ventured into Rapid City.

9. Sioux benefit money refers to funds set aside as payment to landless Sioux. Eligibility applies to those who turned eighteen after the early 1930s, when all available forty-acre sections had been allotted on a per-capita basis.

Some reservations ran out of land to allot at an earlier date. Cheyenne River Reservation is the only reservation that still pays a "per capita" at eighteen. The money derives from funds obtained by the tribe in the Oahe Reservoir settlement.

10. This point Madonna made repeatedly during the interviews. She seemed saddened by the possibility that she infected others and angered because it may have prolonged her own captivity.

11. Although some readers may be surprised that Jay Abdalla was half Syrian, it must be remembered that Lebanese-American

families are not uncommon in South Dakota. Among their better-known members are U.S. Senators James Abouresk and Jim Abnor. Jay said his father was an itinerant hardware salesman traveling the Yankton Sioux reservation and peddling his wares from a horse-drawn wagon and that his mother was a full-blood Yankton.

A majority of the mixed-bloods ("ieska" in Lakota) are of French-Canadian and métis ancestry. French surnames are very common. The majority of Lakota people today are technically mixed bloods. People who are technically full bloods deem this a source of pride and status and grow up learning which families and relatives are full bloods and which mixed bloods. In this writer's opinion the stratification system is much more complex than is actually recognized.

Mixed bloods may fall into two social categories: those who are "Indians," meaning real Indians from the standpoint of cultural behavior; and the real ieska (English speaker), who is culturally "not one of the people" and is generally held in low esteem by the Indians. These racially arbitrary distinctions are critical within the community life of the Lakota reservations. The full bloods seem to be the arbiters of this labeling process.

12. The frozen bodies of those who had died the night before were left outside to be removed for burial. In summer they would be removed to the undertaker immediately. Clearly visible from her window, they were a daily, grim reminder that death was ever present.

13. Madonna stood 5'9" or 5'10" at her full height; for a woman this size to weigh only 120 pounds would have been far below normal.

14. Madonna recalls this experience as one of excruciating agony lasting four or five hours. According to her, placing the hemorrhaging patient in a tub of crushed ice was done in hopes of slowing down the internal bleeding.

15. This yearning to be with her mother is certainly understandable within any cultural context, yet perhaps even more among a people who are largely matriarchal. While the Lakota do not follow a clearly matriarchal pattern, they trace band identity largely through the female side. Historically, women owned the tipi and household goods. Some Lakota still follow a matrilocal pattern after marriage, living for a time in the same home, or close to the home of the mother-in-law. The mature relationship between Madonna and Lucy was one of tremendous mutual respect and affection.

16. It should be remembered here that TB can infect any organ in the body including the skin.

17. Whether Standing Bear's daughter was literally the first Indian patient could not be corroborated. She was, however, one of the first. Not until after 1952 was there any numbering of Indian patients in Sanitor.

18. Judge Sigurd Anderson was governor of South Dakota from 1951 to 1955. Born in 1904 at Arendal, Norway, he immigrated to a farmstead near Canton, South Dakota, in 1907. In a telephone interview on September 5, 1988, the judge recalled those years with a chuckle:

"I must have seen people like Madonna many times each day. . . . Things weren't too good then. . . . I guess I was kind of a pioneer for human rights. I always felt everyone should be treated justly, that we were all equal. At that time there was a growing number of Indian children trying to attend off-reservation schools. Well, in some places that went over fine, but in other places there was a fair amount of resistance.

I can remember telling then Attorney General Ralph Dunham to make sure that Indian children attend the schools they wanted to, and to make sure that the laws concerning equal rights were enforced."

19. Dr. W. L. Meyers was born in 1905 at Jasper, Minnesota, graduated from Creighton University Medical School in December 1935 and assumed his post as Director of Medicine at Custer in 1939. He is survived by his wife, Tina, who provided me with this information by telephone on September 7, 1988.

20. In a telephone interview on September 7, 1988, Lorraine Neville (Madonna's roommate and fellow patient at Custer) described Dr. Meyers as:

. . . someone who took a personal interest in each patient. I had a sister who had tonsils infected with TB. I remember it was Dr. Meyers who took her to Hot Springs for surgery. Taking those tonsils out arrested her TB and probably prevented her from getting active TB. I remember, too, that he could be short tempered. And what he said went! . . . Yes he was truly a good man."

21. The first antitubercular drug used at the sanitorium was INH, Isoniazid.

22. Madonna credits this experience in the sanitorium at Custer with helping her to resolve her own racism. She would say that it helped her to see the good and bad in all people and to give everyone the chance to succeed.

23. Lucy Swan told me this story several times. She would always grin and then cover her mouth at the punch line. In 1973 I took her to Crow Fair and the Custer battlefield, as she looked down at the tree lined river tears came to her eye. Turning, she said, "This is where my mother and father took each other as husband and wife. I have wanted to see this place my whole life." She then turned towards the monument and began to sing in Lakota. Her tears stole the last few phrases. When a tourist asked her what she had sung she answered, "I'm singing for Custer. He was a really brave man." This brings to mind what Lakota elders have told me about the warrior code, that the heroism of a warrior can be measured by the bravery of his enemy.

24. Madonna firmly believes this to be the first lobectomy performed on a TB patient at Sanitor.

25. Olga Huff.

Part Three

1. The inclusion of this vignette came during a May 1990 interview. It is illuminating not only as another example of Madonna's sense of survival but also in regards to racially affected sexual stereotypes of the 1950s. Clearly, Mr. Lewis thought Madonna found him an attractive man, and as a white man he did not greatly fear the consequences even if she reported him. In light of her response and the attitudes still prevailing, it is hardly surprising that she did not discuss it with the jeweler's wife or city police. It is a timely story in light of today's largely unchanged social stereotypes concerning rape.

2. The Old Agency hospital refers to the old Cheyenne River Indian Agency that was covered by the flooding of the Missouri River for the Oahe Reservoir in 1959. Old Agency was across the river from Gettysburg. Eagle Butte now serves as the tribal and BIA headquarters.

3. Shirley Swan and Sidney (Uses The Knife) Keith had a number of children in close sequence. They also experienced their share of trouble early in their marriage. Aside from this it would fit a normal Lakota pattern that Austin, as first-born male or chaske', live for a time with his maternal aunt and grandmother. Alta Keith also spent the first four years of her life with Madonna and Lucy.

4. Commodity food refers to free bulk food distributed by the U.S. Department of Agriculture to poor people. These items include canned butter, chicken, macaroni, rice, flour, and the like. This program exists as part of the price support structure of the USDA.

5. This remarkable narration, quite unusual in published literature, reinforces our human understanding of Madonna's

deepest dreams and hopes. Tuberculosis rendered Madonna unable to conceive, but the core of her personality remained very maternal and flowered fully in her years as a Head Start teacher.

6. Madonna has received the Last Rites of the Catholic church at least seven times in her life. These anointings not only establish a likely record but clearly and poignantly portray the survivalist aspect of her personality, her deep faith in God, and her humor when she speaks of them. The Lakota state that one of their principle cultural values is forbearance or (quiet) long suffering. Madonna's approach to her physical problems seems to personify this value.

7. The Cattle Rehabilitation Program, a ranch business-development program sponsored by the Bureau of Indian Affairs, came to the Cheyenne River Reservation during the early part of Frank Ducheneaux's thirty-year term as chairman.

Ducheneaux remained chairman of a Lakota reservation longer than anyone else in modern history. There are those who consider him to have been a tyrant and political boss; others see the visionary aspects of many of his programs. He seemed to have a self-taught understanding of true economic development, diversifying tribal interests into a grocery store, phone company, ranching, and housing. Furthermore, although he fought constantly with members of the tribe and the council, he was a pioneer in replacing Anglo nonmembers with tribal members in positions of responsibility.

8. Project Head Start is a unique survivor of the Johnson "War on Poverty" era. The program provides preschool enrichment experience for many of our nation's poor children. Community based, it is responsive to local culture, history, and needs. Head Start has been very effective in enhancing early student performance.

Madonna worked as a teacher's aide and then as a teacher and finally as a home-school coordinator for the Cherry Creek Community Head Start Center. It was during her last year as a teacher that I first met her.

9. This writer has heard numerous allegations such as this directed at the Ducheneaux administration. In this particular case it would seem Madonna's version is quite accurate. A Mr. Lindquist was the first attorney who was asked to leave because he was a thorn in the side of the chairman and council. The next to go was a Mr. Dick Churchwell, a South Dakota Legal Aid attorney who handled the case. He told me that the facts of the case were quite clear, and that if he pushed the case strongly enough he would be asked to leave the reservation, which he did. When this took place, in 1973, Ducheneaux was no longer chairman.

10. It would seem that Madonna and Jay were made examples

to reinforce the power of the Rehab committee of the tribal council. Certainly Jay's status as a nonmember placed them in a more vulnerable, and politically weaker position. Because Jay was born to and enrolled in another tribe, he could not vote or take part in the tribal political process or own land on the reservation. This issue of transferring memberships from one Sioux tribe to another remains unresolved. Established formally under the Indian Reorganization Act enacted in 1936, enrollment laws have substantially altered traditional marriage patterns and likely contributed to a sudden rise in a number of inherited diseases such as diabetes and depression.

11. Disenfranchisement, essentially relinquishing one's tribal membership for cash, was occasionally done voluntarily, but the use of it as a threat was a new tactic. Whether an individual can sue his tribe has been resolved by numerous court cases and is ensured by the 1974 Indian Civil Rights Act. This was an emotional issue, especially in light of the horror stories circulating about those tribes that had been legally terminated by the Eisenhower administration.

12. With seasonal unemployment reaching 85 percent, the power of the tribal council to reward or punish tribal members contributes to their power. Loans, jobs, and leases are often granted on an entirely discretional basis. It is a testimony to the solid core of Lakota values and continuity that a government facing these kinds of pressures can function at all. Anglo communities get extremely anxious when unemployment reaches 8 percent, but even during the Depression did not face unemployment rates found perennially on Lakota reservations.

13. This question of "half-breed" versus full blood permeates reservation conversations, politics, and social life. While these hard lines seem less important to those under fifty, it is still an important distinction affecting many aspects of reservation culture and life. The fact that Leonard Cook spoke Lakota placed him in an "Indian" social status, meaning that he was accepted by the full bloods.

14. This vignette gives testimony to Madonna's ambivalent attitude towards race. Her off-reservation experiences had broadened her: On the one hand, she hates "that son of a bitch" who touched her, but on the other, she respects that "hard-working white couple just trying to get a start" and becomes a close friend.

15. Sidney Keith, who was at that time employed by the Indian Health Service as janitor and ambulance driver-attendant, went on to help reestablish the traditional religion and sun dance on the Cheyenne River Reservation. In his own quiet way, Sidney started a renaissance of veneration toward the White Buffalo Calf that has persisted and grown.

16. Madonna made numerous attempts to complete her bachelor's in education. Amassing 136 hours attending part time and summers, she was thwarted more than once by her extremely frail health. Her last attempt to attend college full time was at the University of South Dakota in 1976. She ended up in the hospital. By this time Madonna had to take her oxygen bottle everywhere she went and, as a respiratory cripple, faced constant peril from fatigue, the flu, and common colds.

17. Madonna added this in her final interview in May of 1990. With usual nonexistential cultural candor, she makes a casual, passing remark that the final diagnosis of her encounter with a ghost is a stroke. This is, in fact, understood as a common cultural cause-and-effect relationship. Seeing a ghost may cause a stroke. This effect is called wanag kiteb.

18. This out-of-body or death experience, unusual—perhaps unique—in current Native American literature, shares with stories from other cultures some fairly universal aspects. It is unique in many details, including the round dance with her relatives and the apparition of Levi to escort her across the (universal) crystalline blue river separating the land of the living from that of the dead.

19. As Madonna has stated earlier, this actual or perceived sense of being a pariah never left her. The experiences of the TB sanitorium are so profound that they have affected her self-concept all her life. As a young instructor at the University of South Dakota that fall, I helped Madonna with transportation and her oxygen bottles. I am familiar with all the events related in this book that occurred after 1973. Her tone and the quality of her memory were consistent throughout the taping, whether speaking of the distant past or the events I knew firsthand. These qualities of intelligence, recall, humility, and honesty are the strength of this work.

20. Parts of this vignette were told to me by Austin, who gave permission for their use because, "I want people to know the kind of person Madonna is and the kind of help she has always been to me." Other parts of this vignette are actually stories heard first from Lucy Swan.

21. Refers to uŋgna´ ǵicala hotuŋ (sound of a screech owl). Just as some cultures whistle, stamp their feet, or clap to praise someone or show appreciation, Lakota women have, for as long as their tribal memory, made a particular repetitive, high-pitched, sound called hohńáǵicala hotoŋpi. It is said to be the sound made when warriors returned, or when brave deeds were retold.

Index